I0816682

HOW TO COMPETE

ANCIENT WISDOM FOR MODERN READERS

■ ■ ■ ■

For a full list of titles in the series, go to https://press.princeton.edu/series/ancient-wisdom-for-modern-readers.

How to Compete: An Ancient Guide to the Virtues of Sports
by Lucian

How to Find Happiness: An Ancient Guide to the Good Life
by Marcus Tullius Cicero

How to Be Grateful: An Aztec Guide to the Art of Gratitude
by Pablo of Texcoco

How to Cope: An Ancient Guide to Enduring Hardship
by Boethius

How to Feel: An Ancient Guide to Minding Our Emotions
by the Buddha

How to Be Caring: An Ancient Guide to a Compassionate Life
by Shantideva

How to Make a Home: An Ancient Guide to Style and Comfort
by Vitruvius and Guests

How to Have Willpower: An Ancient Guide to Not Giving In
by Plutarch and Prudentius

How to Talk about Love: An Ancient Guide for Modern Lovers
by Plato

How to Eat: An Ancient Guide for Healthy Living
by a Buffet of Ancient Authors

How to Lose Yourself: An Ancient Guide to Letting Go
by the Buddha and His Followers

HOW TO COMPETE

■ ■ ■ ■ ■

An Ancient Guide to the Virtues of Sports

Lucian

Translated and introduced
by Heather L. Reid and Phillip Mitsis

PRINCETON UNIVERSITY PRESS
PRINCETON AND OXFORD

Published by Princeton University Press
41 William Street, Princeton, New Jersey 08540
99 Banbury Road, Oxford OX2 6JX

press.princeton.edu

GPSR Authorized Representative: Easy Access System Europe - Mustamäe tee 50, 10621 Tallinn, Estonia, gpsr.requests@easproject.com

ISBN 978-0-691-28140-7
ISBN (e-book) 978-0-691-28141-4

Library of Congress Control Number 2025942402

British Library Cataloging-in-Publication Data is available

Editorial: Rob Tempio and Chloe Coy
Production Editorial: Jill Harris
Text Design: Heather Hansen
Jacket Design: Heather Hansen
Publicity: William Pagdatoon and Carmen Jimenez

Jacket image: Relief on pedestal tombstone cure. Pentelic marble, circa 510–500 BC. Finding: Kerameikos in Athens, at Themistokleos walls. National Archaeological Museum of Athens N 3476.

This book has been composed in Stempel Garamond and Adobe Text Pro with Futura Std

Printed in the United States of America

1 3 5 7 9 10 8 6 4 2

For Gareth B. Matthews

1929–2011

CONTENTS

Introduction ix

Anacharsis 3

Glossary 133
Notes 151
Further Reading 165
Acknowledgments 171

INTRODUCTION

Sports are everywhere in modern life. We watch them on our screens, play them in school, and simulate them in video games. Some of us even dedicate years or decades of our lives to competing in pursuit of athletic excellence. But do we really understand sports? How often do we really think about them? When do we ask such basic questions as: Why sports? What is their purpose? Do we take them too seriously? Are sports educational? Do they benefit communities? What, in short, are the virtues of sports?

One way to encourage reflection on the value of sports in a society where athletic

competition and training are so engrained as to remain largely unquestioned might be to pair the perspective of an uninformed outsider with that of a recognized expert. The outsider could ask apparently obvious questions that the expert would have to reflect on and answer with detailed explanations. It might be a philosophical dialogue, humorous yet challenging, informative and entertaining, but most importantly, stimulating of thought and discussion.

Lucian's *Anacharsis* is just that. Though written under Roman rule in the 2nd century CE, it looks back to an even more ancient past, 6th-century-BCE Athens. It pits Solon (630–560 BCE), a legendary lawgiver credited with laying the political foundations for Athens' golden age, against Anacharsis, a quasi-historical sage of the same period who comes from far-away Scythia to learn

about Greek laws and customs. By the time Lucian was writing, Scythia and the figure of Anacharsis were frequently used as literary shorthand for otherness.[1] Their conversation takes place at Athens' Lyceum, a gymnasium[2] that would be recognized by readers as the eventual site of Aristotle's school. It is the perfect place for a philosophical dialogue since philosophers like Socrates were reputed to frequent gymnasiums; indeed, philosophical conversation was a recognized part of gymnasium life throughout Greco-Roman antiquity.[3]

In Lucian's time in the 2nd century CE, gymnasiums remained active and Greek athletics were as popular as ever. Classical philosophy was also back in vogue through a literary and cultural movement called the Second Sophistic.[4] It may have been his society's devotion to Classical philosophy and

sport that motivated Lucian to parody them in "satirical dialogues," a comedic imitation of the Socratic dialogue.[5] Setting *Anacharsis* in a time and place where sport and philosophy were thought to be closely connected enables Lucian to interrogate that connection with critical insight and humor.[6]

Lucian of Samosata was born in Syria around 120 CE, but little else about his biography is certain. His native language was probably Aramaic, but he became a master of Greek oratory and worked both in law courts and as an itinerant lecturer and performer—indeed he may have performed the *Anacharsis* for audiences. He represents himself as turning to philosophy in Athens at the age of 40. At the end of his life, he seems to have been a minor administrator in Roman Egypt. In his numerous essays and dialogues, full of trenchant humor and

philosophical insight, he created a world that reflected the diversity of the Roman Empire and often undercut its social, ethnic, and religious divisions.

In *Anacharsis,* as in several of Lucian's works, the audience is challenged to see the world from a Scythian's outsider perspective. In addition to generating humor, this approach prompts philosophical questioning about aspects of culture that often go uncriticized. Sports and those who compete in them can seem absurd when viewed through unfamiliar eyes. Cricket, for instance, may seem unfathomable and humorous to uninitiated Americans, whereas American football might shock cricket fans with its seemingly unrestrained violence. By offering the perspective of an incredulous and often sarcastic Anacharsis, Lucian prompts reflection not just on the traditions

of ancient Greek sports, but also on their famously competitive mindset.

Why Compete in Sports?

The dialogue begins as Anacharsis observes trainees wrestling in the gymnasium and asks the question "why?" More precisely, he asks *tinos heneka* (for the sake of what) ". . . are your young men doing these things?" (§1). From the standpoint of an outsider, it is very puzzling. Anacharsis recounts that the two men apparently trying to hurt one another now had been amicably rubbing each other down with olive oil just moments before. The paradox cuts to the heart of sport: why do people agree to be challenged, risking pain and even injury, by fellow athletes? How does competition improve individuals and communities? What is the purpose of sport?

"Sport" is actually a modern term, but it covers activities ranging from gym class to the World Cup. "Competition" is a broader term that derives from the Latin *com-petere* ("to strive together"), which corresponds to the Greek "*agōn.*" *Anacharsis* discusses the competitive mindset in activities ranging from education in the gymnasium to trials in the court to the Olympic Games. Even philosophical inquiry, as illustrated by the dialogue itself, adopted the competitive approach integral to Hellenic culture, which was admired and emulated in the Roman Imperial period. In fact, Lucian's Athens was an educational center that attracted people from all over the Empire who wished to absorb traditional Hellenic wisdom.

Just as modern athletes might justify their efforts in terms of the scholarships, sponsorships, or even salaries they hope to receive,

Solon initially justifies sport in terms of its "pleasurable and profitable" rewards (§6). But when the prizes of the most prestigious contests turn out to be leafy crowns, sacred apples, and olive oil, Anacharsis can hardly contain his laughter.[7] He says, sarcastically, that such rewards are "utterly majestic" and worthy of the competitors' seriousness, exertion, and risk of injury, ". . . as if it isn't possible for anyone with a desire for apples to get them without trouble" (§9). Backpedaling, Solon explains that these prizes are merely symbolic; the real reward is the reputation (*doxa*) that follows from victory, adding that the victor is "judged equal to a god" (§10).

Anacharsis remains unconvinced. Does this kind of "pleasure and profit" really compensate for the painful exertion (*ponos*) required? Competitors in the games may be

cheered by thousands of spectators, but from Anacharsis' perspective the presence of so many witnesses only makes the athletes' struggle and suffering more pitiable (§11). The worthlessness of the prizes is compounded by the reality that only very few can hope to receive them. The vast majority of athletes train and suffer in uncertainty, receiving blows and even wounds in competition despite having little chance of victory (§13). One thing is certain however: the monetary value of the prizes does not answer the question, "Why compete in sports?"

Do We Take Sports Too Seriously?

Anacharsis' perspective forces us to question our enthusiasm for sports, which to him seem laughable and pointless (*matēn*). Ancient Greek philosophy frequently warns

against useless or fruitless activity that fails the *tinos heneka* challenge. If I train and compete for the sake of winning valuable prizes, and I fail to win or the prizes turn out to be worthless, then my effort was pointless. Sport, from this perspective, is not worth taking seriously or pursuing with zeal (*spoudē*) as the ancient Athenians do; it is a waste of time and energy. Modern sport philosophy often emphasizes its link to play as something practiced for its own sake without concern for outcomes other than pleasure.[8] This ideal is not espoused in Ancient Greek sport.

Anacharsis is struck by the brutal and bloody nature of the competition he witnesses, which he describes in detail at the start of the dialogue. One person's mouth is so full of blood and sand that it looks like he will be spitting out his teeth, yet a nearby

official does nothing to stop it (§3). Solon assures him that such fighting is "not for the sake of violence" (*hubris*), but Anacharsis shoots back that if *he* were attacked in such a way, he would respond violently with his dagger (§6). The problem is not violence *per se*, but the pointlessness of violence in sports.

Anacharsis points out that assaults like those he saw in the gymnasium would be penalized with large fines in Scythia (§11), and the same could be said today about the aggression witnessed in boxing and mixed martial arts competitions. So why does society permit and even encourage such sports? Their entertainment value is a common answer, but not a persuasive justification. In addition to questioning the sanity of a culture that encourages and even rewards people for fighting each other, Anacharsis worries about spectators who enjoy witnessing such

madness. Not only do these audiences seem to be "neglecting life's necessities" by devoting themselves to sports, but what kind of people feel entertained by watching fellow citizens beat one another to a pulp? (§11).

Solon subsequently adds that spectatorship at quail fights and cockfights is required in Athens (§37), defending the city's seriousness about this and all spectatorship in terms of the competitive mindset it inspires. If Anacharsis were to attend the Olympic, Isthmian, or Panathenaian games in person, Solon says, what he saw there would teach him that the Greeks' zeal for sports is not pointless (§12). By witnessing the many excellences (*aretai*) on display in the games, spectators themselves are said to fall "immoderately in love with excellence and exertions" (§36). Although excellence (*aretē*) is a primary goal in ancient Greek philosophy

and education alike, Anacharsis sees sports as squandering such assets; he thinks those efforts and excellences should be saved for serious purposes like the protection of family and the community (§13).

Are Sports Educational?

Having failed to convince his interlocutor of the virtues of sport by appeal to the prizes or the spectacle of the games, Solon changes gear and attempts to defend its value as education (*paideia*). Anacharsis is delighted by this since he came to Solon expressly to learn about the best form of government, which includes education (§14). Solon warns that to understand the virtues of sport, Anacharsis will have to learn about the entire culture, including religion, family, and "all the rest" (§15). He goes on to describe a "competition shared in common" by the

citizens that rewards their training and exertions with a crown of "human happiness" (*eudaimonia*), which weaves together everything "one might pray to receive from the gods," including freedom, wealth, reputation, and safety (§15). It is an extremely ambitious claim. Although some modern societies still promote sports in education for civic or nationalistic aims, most have more modest goals, such as physical fitness and health.

Solon's explanation prioritizes the mental over the physical benefits of sport for the community. He begins by comparing the city's walls and buildings to its "body," whereas the citizens who govern it are like its "mind." The beauty and safety of city infrastructure is important, he says, but what matters most is that ". . . the citizens might become good with respect to their

minds and strong with respect to their bodies," because such people "will save the city from war and preserve it free and happy" (§20). Education, in other words, works on the body and mind together, challenging them at each appropriate stage of development to produce the competitive mindset that allows the city to flourish.

In §21 Solon recounts a process in which physical exercises combine with intellectual ones in music, arithmetic, writing, and reading. These allow children to learn about "feats of excellence and actions worthy of song," which rouse them to imitation (*mimēsis*). Scholars of ancient sports sometimes overlook this section because it seems irrelevant to them, but ancient Greek athletics is profitably understood as a *mimēsis* of heroic feats (*athla*) that functions educationally by giving participants an embodied

appreciation of heroic *aretē*.[9] In other words, a runner imagining himself as Achilles or a wrestler trying to emulate Heracles comes to learn through training and competition what it means to have excellence worthy of song.

Anacharsis overlooks the connection, begging Solon to continue talking about the mind rather than the "less necessary" exercise and exertion of the body (§21). But Solon continues describing other aspects of Greek *paideia* such as learning the laws, attending the theater, and keeping company with sophists and philosophers who teach the youth ". . . to do what is right, and to engage in the life of the city together in equality, and not to desire shameful things but to aspire toward the good, and to do nothing by force" (§22). By the same token, Solon explains that theatrical *paideia*

celebrates examples of *aretē* and ridicules shameful actions, which spectators are thus motivated to avoid. He concludes his defense of cultural education by saying that "it is by these and all such things that they [the youth] are sharpened with respect to their minds and become better for us" (§23).

Solon then returns to the topic of physical conditioning, making it clear that the benefits of such activities are never merely physical. Sports also train and strengthen the mind to persist in exertions, stand up to blows, and not give in to the fear of being wounded. The two greatest benefits for the city, he says, are that it makes the youth "spirited (*thumoeideis*) and unsparing of their bodies in the face of dangers" (§24). He also mentions health, but almost as an afterthought. It is clear that he regards the educational benefits of sports to be primarily

psychological and that they derive from a *paideia* that combines the cultural celebration of excellence (*aretē*) in drama, literature, and oratory with the opportunity to test one's own *aretē* through competition of various kinds.

Do Sports Benefit Communities?

Though Anacharsis does not interrupt Solon's speech (except to make fun of the comic and tragic actors), one can imagine that he appears unconvinced because, suddenly, Solon switches to a military justification of sport (which Lucian's readers, accustomed to a professional Roman army, might also find unconvincing). War seems to be the one type of *agōn* that Anacharsis takes seriously. Solon argues that wrestling skills are useful in combat, concluding that all such things are supplied "for *that* competition, the one

under arms [since] we consider men trained in this way much better to make use of" (§24). Returning to the theme of utility, he argues that exercise sweats what is "useless and excessive" out of the body, leaving strength and vitality that can be stored up in case of need (§25). Not only will such well-trained men excel under arms, argues Solon, their toned and tanned physiques will strike fear into enemies even when naked (§25).

The idea recalls a story recounted by the Greek historian Diodorus Siculus (12.10.5-6), which suggests that the outnumbered Crotonites credited their victory over the Sybarites to the Pythagorean wrestling champion Milo, whose imposing physical appearance set their enemies to flight. Anacharsis is having none of it, though. He sees sports not as serious education (*paideia*), but rather idle play (*paidia*). He tells Solon,

"If you wish to be free and happy you will need other exercises and true training, the one in arms," adding that those "practicing to be excellent" must not compete "against one another in play but with dangers against those hostile to us" (§32). He then imagines his laughably easy massacre of naked trainees in a gymnasium as they cower and cry in fear behind the columns (§33).[10]

Solon replies that Athenian men do train in arms, but only after they have become "best in their own right" (*aristoi kath' autous*), adding that men so educated make better use of those arms. Indeed, Athenians have no need to carry weapons in their city—unlike Scythia, where lawlessness seems to abound (§34). As Solon explained in §30, in peacetime, Athenians contend not in arms but "in honor over nothing shameful." Their education teaches them to do

"nothing by force," so they pass their time with sports and culture rather than turning towards violence out of idleness. That crown of civic happiness created by the competition shared in common (§15–16) results from the youth being "zealous about what is most beautiful for us" (§30).

To Anacharsis, who still sees gymnasiums, theaters, and stadiums as places for pointless and frivolous pursuits, Athens seems to be carefully preserving its weapons while squandering its young men on useless exertions (§35). When he asks again about the purpose of athletic competitions, Solon offers further civic motivations. They move participants and spectators alike to keep in shape and to be worthy of honors. He says the love of glory (*eukleia*) generated by sports prompts citizens to care about *aretē* and to desire to achieve brilliant things, suggesting that this

competitive mindset is exercised not just in stadiums and gymnasiums, but on the battlefield and, most importantly, in the city itself (§36).

As if to emphasize that his is the moderate position, he offers a more extreme example. Solon points to the Spartans, who were famous even in Roman times for competing in things like enduring the pain of a whip or pushing rival teams off an artificial island. He justifies such activities as the invention of his fellow legendary lawgiver Lycurgus, but he rejects direct imitation of them (§38). Anacharsis remains unconvinced and says he would laugh at the Spartans even more than the Athenians (§39). Solon still does not concede the argument: "Do not think, noble one, that you prevail by default," he warns, without the Spartans having a chance to respond (§40). He adds that since Anacharsis

is unconvinced by Athenian and Spartan *paideia*, he should take his turn and recount the supposedly superior Scythian customs.

How to Make Sense of Sports

At this point we realize that the dialogue itself has been a kind of competition—one that is ending in a draw. This agonistic aspect is easily overlooked, but it may contain the lesson that Lucian is most eager to get across. Philosophical dialogue, like athletic competition, can benefit both participants if it is conducted fairly. In §14, Anacharsis offered to listen passively as Solon explained government and laws—much as audiences were expected to do at sophistic orations. Instead, Solon invites him to enter the gymnasium and sit in the exedra (§16), a location that recalls Socratic-style dialogue.[11] Solon instructs Anacharsis to interrupt and

challenge him in the discussion, so that he may learn from him and thereby benefit Athens. He pushes the point to satirical exaggeration, offering to proclaim his gratitude publicly and set up a statue of Anacharsis alongside those of the Athenian heroes (§17), but the point is made that Athens' brilliance derives at least partly from its citizens' willingness to be challenged and persuaded, even by outsiders.[12]

In §19, Solon invites Anacharsis to be the arbiter of the discussion, setting down guidelines to keep the dialogue from going *exagōnia*, literally outside of the *agōn* (competition). He compares their discussion to trials at the Areopagus aimed at discovering the "naked truth," but reiterates that it is a friendly conversation in the shade of the gymnasium rather than an uninterrupted speech under the sun. The lesson here is that

to make sense of sports we need to think more deeply about them, considering divergent perspectives and articulating the less obvious benefits that they can offer.

Sports are social practices, not natural phenomena beyond our control. Their potential to benefit individuals and communities is great—but hardly automatic. We need to think about sports' potential in our own social and historical contexts, gaining perspective from different ones (as Solon does by describing Sparta's conventions), but never assuming that what works for others will work in the same way for us. Frequently, *Anacharsis* has been read as pure satire, but it also functions as an *aporetic* dialogue, that is, one that leaves us in perplexity. Although offering no clear answers, the kinds of questions it asks are fundamental for thinking about sport. Solon and

Anacharsis agree to continue their conversation the next day. The hope is that readers will do the same, because a friendly competition of thought and discussion with a sense of tolerance and humor is the best way, in the end, to understand the virtues of sports.

HOW TO COMPETE

ΑΝΑΧΑΡΣΙΣ Η ΠΕΡΙ ΓΥΜΝΑΣΙΩΝ

[1] Ταῦτα δὲ ὑμῖν, ὦ Σόλων, τίνος ἕνεκα οἱ νέοι ποιοῦσιν; οἱ μὲν αὐτῶν περιπλεκόμενοι ἀλλήλους ὑποσκελίζουσιν, οἱ δὲ ἄγχουσι καὶ λυγίζουσι καὶ ἐν τῷ πηλῷ συναναφύρονται κυλινδούμενοι ὥσπερ σύες. καίτοι κατʼ ἀρχὰς εὐθὺς ἀποδυσάμενοι—ἑώρων γάρ—λίπα τε ἠλείψαντο καὶ κατέψησε μάλα εἰρηνικῶς ἅτερος τὸν ἕτερον ἐν τῷ μέρει. μετὰ δὲ οὐκ οἶδʼ ὅ τι παθόντες ὠθοῦσί τε ἀλλήλους

ANACHARSIS OR ABOUT NAKED EXERCISE

[1] *Why are your young men doing these things, Solon? Some of them, clinched together, are tripping each other up, while others are choking and twisting as they wallow in the mud, rolling around just like swine.[1] At first, immediately after undressing, they slathered themselves with *olive oil—for I was watching—and took turns very peacefully rubbing one another down. Then I don't know what got into them after that, they are pushing each other with their

---

* Words explained in the glossary are marked by an asterisk on their first occurrence in the translation.

συννενευκότες καὶ τὰ μέτωπα συναράττουσιν ὥσπερ οἱ κριοί.

καὶ ἣν ἰδοὺ ἀράμενος ἐκεινοσὶ τὸν ἕτερον ἐκ τοῖν σκελοῖν ἀφῆκεν εἰς τὸ ἔδαφος, εἶτ᾽ ἐπικαταπεσὼν ἀνακύπτειν οὐκ ἐᾷ, συνωθῶν κάτω εἰς τὸν πηλόν· τέλος δὲ ἤδη περιπλέξας αὐτῷ τὰ σκέλη κατὰ τὴν γαστέρα τὸν πῆχυν ὑποβαλὼν τῷ λαιμῷ ἄγχει ἄθλιον, ὁ δὲ παρακροτεῖ εἰς τὸν ὦμον, ἱκετεύων οἶμαι, ὡς μὴ τέλεον ἀποπνιγείη.

καὶ οὐδὲ τοῦ ἐλαίου ἕνεκα φείδονται μὴ μολύνεσθαι, ἀλλ᾽ ἀφανίσαντες τὸ χρῖμα καὶ τοῦ βορβόρου ἀναπλησθέντες ἐν ἱδρῶτι ἅμα πολλῷ γέλωτα ἐμοὶ γοῦν παρέχουσιν ὥσπερ αἱ ἐγχέλυες ἐκ τῶν χειρῶν διολισθαίνοντες.

heads lowered and butting their foreheads together just like rams.

And look over there, that one is lifting the other one up by the legs and dropping him to the ground. Then, having fallen upon him, he won't let him get up, forcing him down into the mud. Finally now, having clinched him around the belly with his legs while putting his forearm under his neck, he is choking the poor guy, who is slapping his shoulder, surrendering, I think, so that he will not be completely strangled.[2]

Not even for the sake of the olive oil do they spare themselves from getting dirty, but they have ruined their anointment and covered themselves with mire and much *sweat. At the same time, they have provided me at least with much laughter, slithering through one another's hands just like eels.

[2] Ἕτεροι δὲ ἐν τῷ αἰθρίῳ τῆς αὐλῆς τὸ αὐτὸ τοῦτο δρῶσιν, οὐκ ἐν πηλῷ οὗτοί γε, ἀλλὰ ψάμμον ταύτην βαθεῖαν ὑποβαλόμενοι ἐν τῷ ὀρύγματι πάττουσίν τε ἀλλήλους καὶ αὐτοὶ ἑκόντες ἐπαμῶνται τὴν κόνιν ἀλεκτρυόνων δίκην, ὡς ἀφυκτότεροι εἶεν ἐν ταῖς συμπλοκαῖς, οἶμαι, τῆς ψάμμου τὸν ὄλισθον ἀφαιρούσης καὶ βεβαιοτέραν ἐν ξηρῷ παρεχούσης τὴν ἀντίληψιν.

[3] Οἱ δὲ ὀρθοστάδην κεκονιμένοι καὶ αὐτοὶ παίουσιν ἀλλήλους προσπεσόντες καὶ λακτίζουσιν. οὑτοσὶ γοῦν καὶ τοὺς ὀδόντας ἔοικεν ἀποπτύσειν ὁ κακοδαίμων, οὕτως αἵματος αὐτῷ καὶ ψάμμου ἀναπέπλησται τὸ στόμα, πύξ, ὡς ὁρᾷς, παταχθέντος εἰς τὴν γνάθον. ἀλλ᾽ οὐδὲ ὁ ἄρχων οὑτοσὶ διίστησιν αὐτοὺς καὶ λύει τὴν μάχην—τεκμαίρομαι γὰρ τῇ πορφυρίδι τῶν ἀρχόντων τινὰ τοῦτον

[2] Others in the open-air of the courtyard are doing the exact same thing, but at least those are not in mud. Rather, having put down deep sand in a pit, they are sprinkling it on each other. They purposely heap *dust upon themselves in the manner of roosters, so that they might be harder to escape from in clinches. The sand takes away the slipperiness, I think, and creates a dry surface for a firmer grip.

[3] And those over there standing upright, covered in dust as well, having lunged against each other, are hitting and kicking. Indeed, that one there looks like he will be spitting out his teeth, the poor guy. His mouth has been filled with blood and sand since, as you see, he was struck on the jaw with a fist. But not even that official is separating them and stopping the fight—I surmise from the purple that this is one of the

εἶναι—ὁ δὲ καὶ ἐποτρύνει καὶ τὸν πατάξαντα ἐπαινεῖ.

[4] Ἄλλοι δὲ ἀλλαχόθι πάντες ἐγκονοῦσι καὶ ἀναπηδῶσιν ὥσπερ θέοντες ἐπὶ τοῦ αὐτοῦ μένοντες καὶ εἰς τὸ ἄνω συναλλόμενοι λακτίζουσιν τὸν ἀέρα.

[5] Ταῦτα οὖν ἐθέλω εἰδέναι τίνος ἀγαθοῦ ἂν εἴη ποιεῖν· ὡς ἔμοιγε μανίᾳ μᾶλλον ἐοικέναι δοκεῖ τὸ πρᾶγμα, καὶ οὐκ ἔστιν ὅστις ἂν ῥᾳδίως μεταπείσειέ με ὡς οὐ παραπαίουσιν οἱ ταῦτα δρῶντες.

ΣΟΛΩΝ

[6] Καὶ εἰκότως, ὦ Ἀνάχαρσι, τοιαῦτά σοι τὰ γιγνόμενα φαίνεται, ξένα γε ὄντα καὶ πάμπολυ τῶν Σκυθικῶν ἐθῶν ἀπᾴδοντα, καθάπερ καὶ ὑμῖν πολλὰ εἰκὸς εἶναι μαθήματα καὶ ἐπιτηδεύματα τοῖς Ἕλλησιν ἡμῖν ἀλλόκοτα εἶναι δόξαντα ἄν, εἴ τις ἡμῶν ὥσπερ σὺ νῦν ἐπισταίη αὐτοῖς. πλὴν ἀλλὰ θάρρει, ὦγαθέ· οὐ

men in charge—rather, he even urges and praises the one who has landed the blows.[3]

[4] In other places all the rest are hustling about and jumping up, as if running while staying in the same place and leaping up together kicking the air.

[5] I want to know what good it would be to do these things. To me at least, the activity seems more like madness,[4] and there is no one who could easily convince me that those doing these things are not out of their minds.

Solon

[6] And it is plausible, Anacharsis, that the things taking place appear to you as such insofar as they are foreign and thoroughly out of tune with Scythian traditions—just like many of your doctrines and practices would probably seem strange to us Hellenes, if one of us, as you are now, were to

γὰρ μανία τὰ γιγνόμενά ἐστιν οὐδ᾽ ἐφ᾽ ὕβρει οὗτοι παίουσιν ἀλλήλους καὶ κυλίουσιν ἐν τῷ πηλῷ ἢ ἐπιπάττουσιν τὴν κόνιν, ἀλλ᾽ ἔχει τινὰ χρείαν οὐκ ἀτερπῆ τὸ πρᾶγμα καὶ ἀκμὴν οὐ μικρὰν ἐπάγει τοῖς σώμασιν· ἢν γοῦν ἐνδιατρίψῃς, ὥσπερ οἶμαί σε ποιήσειν, τῇ Ἑλλάδι, οὐκ εἰς μακρὰν εἷς καὶ αὐτὸς ἔσῃ τῶν πεπηλωμένων ἢ κεκονιμένων· οὕτω σοι τὸ πρᾶγμα ἡδύ τε ἅμα καὶ λυσιτελὲς εἶναι δόξει.

ΑΝΑΧΑΡΣΙΣ

Ἄπαγε, ὦ Σόλων, ὑμῖν ταῦτα γένοιτο τὰ ὠφέλιμα καὶ τερπνά, ἐμὲ δὲ εἴ τις ὑμῶν τοιοῦτό τι διαθείη, εἴσεται ὡς οὐ μάτην παρεζώσμεθα τὸν [7] ἀκινάκην. ἀτὰρ εἰπέ μοι,

become acquainted with them. Nevertheless, take heart my good man; for the things taking place are not madness, nor is it for the sake of *violence that they are hitting each other and rolling around in the mud or sprinkling dust on one another. Rather the activity has a particular utility, which is not without enjoyment and brings their bodies to a not insignificant peak. Indeed, if you spend time in Greece, as I think you will, before long you yourself will be one of the muddy and dusty as well—the activity will seem that pleasurable and at the same time profitable to you.

Anacharsis

No thanks, Solon, these things might be beneficial and enjoyable for you people, but if one of you treats me like this, he will find out that we do not strap on the [7] dagger[5]

τί ὄνομα ἔθεσθε τοῖς γιγνομένοις, ἢ τί φῶμεν ποιεῖν αὐτούς;

ΣΟΛΩΝ

Ὁ μὲν χῶρος αὐτός, ὦ Ἀνάχαρσι, γυμνάσιον ὑφ᾽ ἡμῶν ὀνομάζεται καὶ ἔστιν ἱερὸν Ἀπόλλωνος τοῦ Λυκείου. καὶ τὸ ἄγαλμα δὲ αὐτοῦ ὁρᾷς, τὸν ἐπὶ τῇ στήλῃ κεκλιμένον, τῇ ἀριστερᾷ μὲν τὸ τόξον ἔχοντα, ἡ δεξιὰ δὲ ὑπὲρ τῆς κεφαλῆς [8] ἀνακεκλασμένη ὥσπερ ἐκ καμάτου μακροῦ ἀναπαυόμενον δείκνυσι τὸν θεόν. τῶν γυμνασμάτων δὲ τούτων τὸ μὲν ἐν τῷ πηλῷ ἐκεῖνο πάλη καλεῖται, οἱ δ᾽ ἐν τῇ κόνει παλαίουσι καὶ αὐτοί, τὸ δὲ παίειν ἀλλήλους ὀρθοστάδην παγκρατιάζειν λέγομεν. καὶ ἄλλα δὲ ἡμῖν ἐστι γυμνάσια τοιαῦτα πυγμῆς καὶ δίσκου καὶ τοῦ ὑπεράλλεσθαι, ὧν ἁπάντων ἀγῶνας προτίθεμεν, καὶ ὁ κρατήσας ἄριστος

*pointlessly. Anyway, tell me, what name do you give to these things taking place, or what should we say they are doing?

Solon

The place itself, Anacharsis, is called by us *"gymnasium," and it is a sacred place dedicated to Apollo of the *Lyceum. You see the wondrous statue of him leaning against a stone pillar, holding a bow in his left hand while the right is bent back over his head, [8] portraying the god as if resting from a long *effort.[6] As for the *exercises, that one in the mud is called *"wrestling," and the ones in the dust, they too are wrestling, and we call hitting each other while standing *"*pankration*." We also have other such exercises—*boxing and *discus and *jumping—for all of which we set up

εἶναι δοκεῖ τῶν καθ᾽ αὑτὸν καὶ ἀναιρεῖται τὰ ἆθλα.

ΑΝΑΧΑΡΣΙΣ

[9] Τὰ δὲ ἆθλα τίνα ὑμῖν ταῦτά ἐστιν;

ΣΟΛΩΝ

Ὀλυμπίασι μὲν στέφανος ἐκ κοτίνου, Ἰσθμοῖ δὲ ἐκ πίτυος, ἐν Νεμέᾳ δὲ σελίνων πεπλεγμένος, Πυθοῖ δὲ μῆλα τῶν ἱερῶν τοῦ θεοῦ, παρ᾽ ἡμῖν δὲ τοῖς Παναθηναίοις τὸ ἔλαιον τὸ ἐκ τῆς μορίας. τί ἐγέλασας, ὦ Ἀνάχαρσι; ἢ διότι μικρά σοι εἶναι ταῦτα δοκεῖ;

ΑΝΑΧΑΡΣΙΣ

Οὔκ, ἀλλὰ πάνσεμνα, ὦ Σόλων, κατέλεξας τὰ ἆθλα καὶ ἄξια τοῖς τε διαθεῖσιν αὐτὰ φιλοτιμεῖσθαι ἐπὶ τῇ μεγαλοδωρεᾷ καὶ τοῖς

*competitions, and the one who prevails is believed to be the *best among his peers and carries off the *prizes.

Anacharsis

[9] And what are your prizes?

Solon

At the Olympics, a crown woven from wild olive, at the Isthmian of pine, in the Nemean of wild celery;[7] at the Pythian, apples from the god's sacred grounds,[8] and for us at the Panathenaian, olive oil from the sacred grove.[9] Why did you laugh, Anacharsis? Or is it because these seem insignificant to you?

Anacharsis

No, Solon, the prizes you have recounted are utterly majestic, and worthy not only for those distributing them to contend in honor

ἀγωνισταῖς αὐτοῖς ὑπερεσπουδακέναι περὶ τὴν ἀναίρεσιν τῶν τηλικούτων, ὥστε μήλων ἕνεκα καὶ σελίνων τοσαῦτα προπονεῖν καὶ κινδυνεύειν ἀγχομένους πρὸς ἀλλήλων καὶ κατακλωμένους, ὡς οὐκ ἐνὸν ἀπραγμόνως εὐπορῆσαι μήλων ὅτῳ ἐπιθυμία ἢ σελίνῳ ἐστεφανῶσθαι ἢ πίτυϊ μήτε πηλῷ καταχριόμενον τὸ πρόσωπον μήτε λακτιζόμενον εἰς τὴν γαστέρα ὑπὸ τῶν ἀνταγωνιστῶν.

ΣΟΛΩΝ

[10] Ἀλλ', ὦ ἄριστε, οὐκ εἰς ψιλὰ τὰ διδόμενα ἡμεῖς ἀποβλέπομεν. ταῦτα μὲν γάρ ἐστι σημεῖα τῆς νίκης καὶ γνωρίσματα οἵτινες οἱ κρατήσαντες. ἡ δὲ παρακολουθοῦσα τούτοις δόξα τοῦ παντὸς ἀξία τοῖς νενικηκόσιν, ὑπὲρ ἧς καὶ λακτίζεσθαι καλῶς ἔχει τοῖς θηρωμένοις

over their lavishness, but also for the competitors themselves to be so zealous about carrying off such important things that for the sake of apples and wild celery they undergo such hard exertions beforehand and run the risk of being choked and crushed by one another.[10] As if it isn't possible for anyone with a desire for apples to get them without trouble, or to be crowned with celery or pine without their face being smeared with mud or being kicked in the stomach by their *antagonists.

Solon

[10] But we, best of men, do not pay attention to what is given *per se.* For these are merely symbols of *victory and tokens of recognition secured by the ones who have prevailed. It is the reputation that follows from these that is worth everything to the

τὴν εὔκλειαν ἐκ τῶν πόνων. οὐ γὰρ ἀπονητὶ προσγένοιτο ἂν αὕτη, ἀλλὰ χρὴ τὸν ὀρεγόμενον αὐτῆς πολλὰ τὰ δυσχερῆ ἀνασχόμενον ἐν τῇ ἀρχῇ τότ' ἤδη τὸ λυσιτελὲς καὶ ἡδὺ τέλος ἐκ τῶν καμάτων περιμένειν.

ΑΝΑΧΑΡΣΙΣ

Τοῦτο φής, ὦ Σόλων, τὸ τέλος ἡδὺ καὶ λυσιτελές, ὅτι πάντες αὐτοὺς ὄψονται ἐστεφανωμένους καὶ ἐπὶ τῇ νίκῃ ἐπαινέσονται πολὺ πρότερον οἰκτείραντες ἐπὶ ταῖς πληγαῖς, οἱ δὲ εὐδαιμονήσουσιν ἀντὶ τῶν πόνων μῆλα καὶ σέλινα ἔχοντες.

victorious. To those hunting glory from their *exertions, even being kicked is good on account of it. For it [glory][†] doesn't come without exertion, rather it is necessary for the one desiring it to bear many difficulties in the beginning and only then to expect the profitable and pleasurable end of their efforts.

Anacharsis

So you are telling me, Solon, that this end is pleasurable and profitable because everyone will see them [the athletes] crowned and will praise them for their victory—having pitied them much earlier for the blows—and that they will be *happy having apples and celery in exchange for their exertions.

[†] Bracketed words are not in the Greek text, but are added here for clarification.

ΣΟΛΩΝ

Ἄπειρος εἶ, φημί, τῶν ἡμετέρων ἔτι· μετὰ μικρὸν δὲ ἄλλα σοι δόξει περὶ αὐτῶν, ἐπειδὰν εἰς τὰς πανηγύρεις ἀπιὼν ὁρᾷς τοσοῦτο πλῆθος ἀνθρώπων συλλεγόμενον ἐπὶ τὴν θέαν τῶν τοιούτων καὶ θέατρα μυρίανδρα συμπληρούμενα καὶ τοὺς ἀγωνιστὰς ἐπαινουμένους, τὸν δὲ καὶ νικήσαντα αὐτῶν ἰσόθεον νομιζόμενον.

ΑΝΑΧΑΡΣΙΣ

[11] Αὐτὸ τοῦτο, ὦ Σόλων, καὶ τὸ οἴκτιστόν ἐστιν, εἰ μὴ ἐπ᾽ ὀλίγων ταῦτα πάσχουσιν, ἀλλὰ ἐν τοσούτοις θεαταῖς καὶ μάρτυσι τῆς ὕβρεως, οἳ δηλαδὴ εὐδαιμονίζουσιν αὐτοὺς αἵματι ῥαινομένους ὁρῶντες ἢ ἀγχομένους ὑπὸ τῶν ἀντιπάλων· ταῦτα γὰρ τὰ εὐδαιμονέστατα πρόσεστι τῇ νίκῃ αὐτῶν.

Solon

You are still unacquainted with our ways, I think. But after a little while these things will seem different to you, whenever you go to the festivals and see such a great crowd of people gathered together to view these sorts of things, and venues for 10,000 people completely filled, the competitors being praised, and the victor among them judged equal to a god.

Anacharsis

[11] But this is the very thing that is most pitiable, Solon, if they suffer these things not in the presence of a few, but among so many *spectators and witnesses of the violence. They no doubt consider them [the athletes] happy when they see them spattered with blood and choked by their adversaries; for these are the greatest blessings attached to

παρ᾽ ἡμῖν δὲ τοῖς Σκύθαις ἤν τις, ὦ Σόλων, ἢ πατάξῃ τινὰ τῶν πολιτῶν ἢ ἀνατρέψῃ προσπεσὼν ἢ θοἰμάτια περιρρήξῃ, μεγάλας οἱ πρεσβῦται τὰς ζημίας ἐπάγουσι, κἂν ἐπ᾽ ὀλίγων μαρτύρων τοῦτο πάθῃ τις, οὔτι γε ἐν τηλικούτοις θεάτροις, οἷα σὺ διηγῇ τὸ Ἰσθμοῖ καὶ τὸ ἐν Ὀλυμπίᾳ.

οὐ μὴν ἀλλὰ τοὺς μὲν ἀγωνιστὰς οἰκτείρειν μοι ἔπεισιν ὧν πάσχουσιν, τῶν δὲ θεατῶν οὓς φὴς ἁπανταχόθεν τοὺς ἀρίστους παραγίγνεσθαι εἰς τὰς πανηγύρεις καὶ πάνυ θαυμάζω, εἰ τἀναγκαῖα παρέντες σχολάζουσιν ἐπὶ τοῖς τοιούτοις. οὐδὲ γὰρ ἐκεῖνό πω δύναμαι κατανοῆσαι ὅ τι τὸ τερπνὸν αὐτοῖς, ὁρᾶν παιομένους τε καὶ διαπληκτιζομένους ἀνθρώπους καὶ πρὸς τὴν γῆν ἀραττομένους καὶ συντριβομένους ὑπ᾽ ἀλλήλων.

their victory. But among us Scythians, Solon, if anyone were to strike one of the citizens or, having attacked him, flip him over or tear off his cloak, the elders would impose large fines, even if someone suffers this before a few witnesses, much less in such great venues of the sort you describe on the Isthmus and in Olympia.

Entirely to the contrary, the things the competitors suffer lead me to pity them. And I very much wonder at the spectators attending the festivals, whom you say are the best people from all over, whether they are neglecting life's necessities by devoting themselves to such things. For I am not yet able to fully understand what enjoyment they get from seeing people hit and grabbed and then thrown to the ground and beaten to a pulp by each other.

ΣΟΛΩΝ

[12] Εἰ καιρὸς ἦν, ὦ Ἀνάχαρσι, Ὀλυμπίων ἢ Ἰσθμίων ἢ Παναθηναίων, αὐτὸ ἄν σε τὸ γιγνόμενον ἐδίδαξεν ὡς οὐ μάτην ἐσπουδάκαμεν ἐπὶ τούτοις. οὐ γὰρ οὕτω λέγων ἄν τις προσβιβάσειέν σε τῇ ἡδονῇ τῶν ἐκεῖ δρωμένων, ὡς εἰ καθεζόμενος αὐτὸς ἐν μέσοις τοῖς θεαταῖς βλέποις ἀρετὰς ἀνδρῶν καὶ κάλλη σωμάτων καὶ εὐεξίας θαυμαστὰς καὶ ἐμπειρίας δεινὰς καὶ ἰσχὺν ἄμαχον καὶ τόλμαν καὶ φιλοτιμίαν καὶ γνώμας ἀηττήτους καὶ σπουδὴν ἄλεκτον ὑπὲρ τῆς νίκης. εὖ γὰρ δὴ οἶδα ὡς οὐκ ἂν ἐπαύσω ἐπαινῶν καὶ ἐπιβοῶν καὶ ἐπικροτῶν.

Solon

[12] If it were the appropriate time, Anacharsis, for the Olympic, Isthmian, or Panathenaian games, the events taking place there would teach you that we have not been pointlessly zealous about them. For not by merely talking this way could someone bring you close to experiencing the pleasure of what is done there—as if, taking a seat amidst the spectators yourself, you were to see the *excellences of men and the beauty of their bodies and their wonderful *fitness and their tremendous skills and unbeatable strength and daring and love of honor and unconquerable resolve and indescribable zeal for victory. At any rate, I know very well indeed that you would not stop praising and shouting and cheering.

ΑΝΑΧΑΡΣΙΣ

[13] Νὴ Δί', ὦ Σόλων, καὶ ἐπιγελῶν γε προσέτι καὶ ἐπιχλευάζων· ἅπαντα γὰρ ὁπόσα κατηριθμήσω ἐκεῖνα, τὰς ἀρετὰς καὶ τὰς εὐεξίας καὶ τὰ κάλλη καὶ τόλμαν, ὁρῶ οὐδενὸς μεγάλου ἕνεκα παραπολλυμένας ὑμῖν, οὔτε πατρίδος κινδυνευούσης οὔτε χώρας πορθουμένης οὔτε φίλων ἢ οἰκείων πρὸς ὕβριν ἀπαγομένων. ὥστε τοσούτῳ γελοιότεροι ἂν εἶεν, ἄριστοι μέν, ὡς φής, ὄντες, μάτην δὲ τοσαῦτα πάσχοντες καὶ ταλαιπωρούμενοι καὶ αἰσχύνοντες τὰ κάλλη καὶ τὰ μεγέθη τῇ ψάμμῳ καὶ τοῖς ὑπωπίοις, ὡς μήλου καὶ κοτίνου ἐγκρατεῖς γένοιντο νικήσαντες. ἡδὺ γάρ μοι ἀεὶ μεμνῆσθαι τῶν ἄθλων τοιούτων ὄντων. ἀτὰρ εἰπέ μοι, πάντες αὐτὰ λαμβάνουσιν οἱ ἀγωνισταί;

Anacharsis

[13] Oh yes, by Zeus, and on top of that, Solon, laughing and jeering, because all the many things you enumerated—the excellences and the fitness and the beauties and the daring—I see them being wasted by you for the sake of nothing great. For neither is your fatherland in danger, nor are your lands being plundered, nor are your friends and family being violently abducted. Consequently, being the best as you say, they would be that much more ridiculous suffering so much pointlessly and undergoing hardship and disfiguring their beauty and physiques with sand and black eyes in order to become victors in possession of apples and wild olive. For it is pleasant to me to continually mention the prizes, they being of this sort. Anyway, tell me, do all the competitors receive them?

ΣΟΛΩΝ

Οὐδαμῶς, ἀλλὰ εἷς ἐξ ἁπάντων, ὁ κρατήσας αὐτῶν.

ΑΝΑΧΑΡΣΙΣ

Εἶτα, ὦ Σόλων, ἐπὶ τῷ ἀδήλῳ καὶ ἀμφιβόλῳ τῆς νίκης τοσοῦτοι πονοῦσι, καὶ ταῦτ᾽ εἰδότες ὅτι ὁ μὲν νικῶν εἷς ἔσται πάντως, οἱ δὲ ἡττώμενοι πάμπολλοι, μάτην ἄθλιοι πληγάς, οἱ δὲ καὶ τραύματα λαμβάνοντες;

ΣΟΛΩΝ

[14] Ἔοικας, ὦ Ἀνάχαρσι, μηδέπω ἐννενοηκέναι πολιτείας ὀρθῆς πέρι μηδέν· οὐ γὰρ ἂν τὰ κάλλιστα τῶν ἐθῶν ἐν ψόγῳ ἐτίθεσο. ἢν δέ σοι μελήσῃ ποτὲ εἰδέναι ὅπως ἂν τὰ κάλλιστα οἰκηθείη πόλις καὶ ὅπως ἂν ἄριστοι γένοιντο οἱ πολῖται αὐτῆς, ἐπαινέσῃ

Solon

Not at all, but out of all of them, one—the one who has prevailed over the others.

Anacharsis

And so, Solon, do they exert themselves to such an extent for the uncertainty and doubtfulness of victory,[11] knowing that in any case there will be one victor, but very many defeated—miserable[12] fellows pointlessly receiving blows, some even wounds?

Solon

[14] Anacharsis, it looks like you have not yet reflected on a correct form of government at all; otherwise you would not be reproaching the most *beautiful of traditions. If it should ever be your concern to learn how a city is most beautifully managed and

ιύιε καὶ τὰς ἀσκήσεις ταύτας καὶ τὴν φιλοτιμίαν ἣν φιλοτιμούμεθα περὶ αὐτάς, καὶ εἴσῃ ὅτι πολὺ τὸ χρήσιμον ἔχουσιν ἐγκαταμεμιγμένον τοῖς πόνοις, εἰ καὶ νῦν μάτην σπουδάζεσθαι δοκοῦσιν.

ΑΝΑΧΑΡΣΙΣ

Καὶ μήν, ὦ Σόλων, κατ᾽ οὐδὲν ἄλλο ἀπὸ τῆς Σκυθίας ἥκω παρ᾽ ὑμᾶς τοσαύτην μὲν γῆν διοδεύσας, μέγαν δὲ τὸν Εὔξεινον καὶ δυσχείμερον περαιωθείς, ἢ ὅπως νόμους τε τοὺς Ἑλλήνων ἐκμάθοιμι καὶ ἔθη <τὰ> παρ᾽ ὑμῖν κατανοήσαιμι καὶ πολιτείαν τὴν ἀρίστην ἐκμελετήσαιμι. διὸ καὶ σὲ μάλιστα φίλον ἐξ ἁπάντων Ἀθηναίων καὶ ξένον προειλόμην κατὰ κλέος, ἐπείπερ ἤκουον νόμων τε

how its citizens become best, you would then praise both this kind of *training and the *love of honor with which we contend over these things. You would also understand that there is much that is useful mixed in with their exertions, even if they now seem to be zealous pointlessly.

Anacharsis

To be sure, Solon, for no other reason have I have come to you people from Scythia—having traversed such a vast expanse of the world and crossing the great and stormy Black Sea—than to get to know the laws of the Hellenes and to thoroughly understand the traditions among you and to carefully study the best form of government. And for that reason, I deliberately chose you in particular out of all the Athenians to be my friend and host because of your renown—especially

συγγραφέα τινὰ εἶναί σε καὶ ἐθῶν τῶν ἀρίστων εὑρετὴν καὶ ἐπιτηδευμάτων ὠφελίμων εἰσηγητήν, καὶ ὅλως πολιτείας τινὸς συναρμοστήν. ὥστε οὐκ ἂν φθάνοις διδάσκων με καὶ μαθητὴν ποιούμενος· ὡς ἔγωγε ἡδέως ἂν ἄσιτός σοι καὶ ἄποτος παρακαθεζόμενος, εἰς ὅσον ἂν αὐτὸς διαρκοίης λέγων, κεχηνὼς ἐπακούοιμι περὶ πολιτείας τε καὶ νόμων διεξιόντος.

ΣΟΛΩΝ

[15] Τὰ μὲν πάντα οὐ ῥᾴδιον, ὦ ἑταῖρε, διελθεῖν ἐν βραχεῖ, ἀλλὰ κατὰ μέρη ἐπιὼν εἴσῃ ἕκαστα, οἷα μὲν περὶ θεῶν, οἷα δὲ περὶ γονέων ἢ περὶ γάμων ἢ τῶν ἄλλων δοκεῖ ἡμῖν. ἃ δὲ περὶ τῶν νέων γιγνώσκομεν καὶ ὅπως αὐτοῖς χρώμεθα, ἐπειδὰν πρῶτον ἄρξωνται συνιέναι τε τοῦ βελτίονος καὶ τῷ σώματι ἀνδρίζεσθαι

since I used to hear that you were an author of laws, a founder of the best traditions, and one who introduced beneficial practices; in short, one who put together a particular form of government. So do not delay teaching me and making me your student. For my part, I would sit with pleasure beside you without food and drink for however long you yourself persist in speaking. With mouth agape, I would listen as you go through both the government and laws.

Solon

[15] It is not easy to go through all these things briefly, my friend, but approaching the parts individually you will come to know each of the sorts of things we believe about the gods, or about parents or marriage or all the rest. What we recognize about young men and how we make use of them

καὶ ὑφίστασθαι τοὺς πόνους, ταῦτα ἤδη σοι διέξειμι, ὡς μάθοις οὗτινος χάριν τὰς ἀσκήσεις ταύτας προτεθείκαμεν αὐτοῖς καὶ διαπονεῖν τὸ σῶμα καταναγκάζομεν, οὐ μόνον ἕνεκα τῶν ἀγώνων, ὅπως τὰ ἆθλα δύναιντο ἀναιρεῖσθαι—ἐπ᾽ ἐκεῖνα μὲν γὰρ ὀλίγοι πάνυ ἐξ ἁπάντων χωροῦσιν—ἀλλὰ μεῖζόν τι ἁπάσῃ τῇ πόλει ἀγαθὸν ἐκ τούτου καὶ αὐτοῖς ἐκείνοις προσκτώμενοι. κοινὸς γάρ τις ἀγὼν ἄλλος ἅπασι τοῖς ἀγαθοῖς πολίταις πρόκειται καὶ στέφανος οὐ πίτυος οὐδὲ κοτίνου ἢ σελίνων, ἀλλ᾽ ὃς ἐν αὑτῷ συλλαβὼν ἔχει τὴν ἀνθρώπου εὐδαιμονίαν, οἷον ἐλευθερίαν λέγω αὐτοῦ τε ἑκάστου ἰδίᾳ καὶ κοινῇ τῆς πατρίδος καὶ πλοῦτον καὶ δόξαν καὶ ἑορτῶν πατρίων ἀπόλαυσιν καὶ οἰκείων σωτηρίαν, καὶ συνόλως

whenever they first start to become aware of what is better and to reach manhood physically and to undertake exertions, I will go through for you now. That way you might learn for what purpose we have set up training for them and force them to strenuously exert the *body. It is not only for the sake of the competitions, so that they might be able to carry off prizes—for very few out of all of them get that far—but additionally they gain from it some greater good for the whole city and for themselves. For another competition shared in common lies before all the good citizens, and a crown not of pine or wild olive or celery, but one that brings together in itself all of human *happiness.[13] I mean by this the *freedom of each person individually and of the fatherland in common, and wealth and reputation and enjoyment of ancestral festivals, and safety of the

ιὰ κάλλιστα ὧν ἄν τις εὔξαιτο γενέσθαι οἱ παρὰ τῶν θεῶν. ταῦτα πάντα τῷ στεφάνῳ ὅν φημι συναναπέπλεκται καὶ ἐκ τοῦ ἀγῶνος ἐκείνου περιγίγνεται ἐφ᾽ ὃν αἱ ἀσκήσεις αὗται καὶ οἱ πόνοι ἄγουσιν.

ΑΝΑΧΑΡΣΙΣ

[16] Εἶτα, ὦ θαυμάσιε Σόλων, τοιαῦτά μοι καὶ τηλικαῦτα ἔχων ἆθλα διεξιέναι, μῆλα καὶ σέλινα διηγοῦ καὶ θαλλὸν ἐλαίας ἀγρίας καὶ πίτυν;

ΣΟΛΩΝ

Καὶ μήν, ὦ Ἀνάχαρσι, οὐδ᾽ ἐκεῖνά σοι ἔτι δόξει μικρὰ εἶναι, ὁπόταν ἃ λέγω καταμάθῃς· ἀπὸ γάρ τοι τῆς αὐτῆς γνώμης γίγνεται, καὶ μέρη πάντα ταῦτά ἐστι μικρὰ τοῦ μείζονος ἐκείνου ἀγῶνος καὶ τοῦ στεφάνου ὃν κατέλεξα τοῦ πανευδαίμονος. ὁ δὲ λόγος, οὐκ οἶδ᾽ ὅπως

family, which taken together are the most beautiful things one might pray to receive from the gods. All these have been woven together in the crown I am speaking of and result from that competition toward which this training and the exertions lead.

Anacharsis

[16] And yet, wondrous Solon, having these and such great prizes to go through for me, you describe apples and celery and a sprig of wild olive and pine?

Solon

To be sure, Anacharsis, not even these [prizes] will still seem insignificant to you once you closely examine what I am saying; for they arise from the same intent and are all small parts of that great competition and of the crown of complete happiness that I

ὑπερβὰς τὴν τάξιν, ἐκείνων πρότερον ἐπεμνήσθη τῶν Ἰσθμοῖ γιγνομένων καὶ Ὀλυμπίασι καὶ ἐν Νεμέᾳ. πλὴν ἀλλὰ νώ—σχολὴν γὰρ ἄγομεν καὶ σύ, ὡς φής, προθυμῇ ἀκούειν—ἀναδραμούμεθα ῥᾳδίως πρὸς τὴν ἀρχὴν καὶ τὸν κοινὸν ἀγῶνα δι᾽ ὅν φημι πάντα ταῦτα ἐπιτηδεύεσθαι.

ΑΝΑΧΑΡΣΙΣ

Ἄμεινον, ὦ Σόλων, οὕτως· καθ᾽ ὁδὸν γὰρ ἂν ἡμῖν ὁ λόγος μᾶλλον προχωροίη, καὶ τάχ᾽ ἂν ἴσως ἀπὸ τούτων πεισθείην μηδὲ ἐκείνων ἔτι καταγελᾶν, εἴ τινα ἴδοιμι σεμνυνόμενον κοτίνῳ ἢ σελίνῳ ἐστεφανωμένον. ἀλλ᾽ εἰ δοκεῖ, εἰς τὸ σύσκιον ἐκεῖσε ἀπελθόντες καθίσωμεν ἐπὶ τῶν θάκων, ὡς μὴ ἐνοχλοῖεν

recounted. Our discussion, I'm not sure how, transgressed the proper order and mentioned first of all those events taking place in the Isthmian and Olympic and Nemean games. Nevertheless—since we are at leisure and you, as you say, are eager to hear—it is easy for the two of us to return to the beginning and to that shared competition I am speaking of for which all of these things are practiced.

Anacharsis

It would be better that way, Solon, for our discussion would make more progress step by step, and perhaps I would be persuaded by what you are saying to never again mock someone were I to see them being proud for having been crowned with wild olive or celery. But if you agree, let us sit down on the

ἡμῖν <οἱ> ἐπικεκραγότες τοῖς παλαίουσιν. ἄλλως τε—εἰρήσεται γάρ—οὐδὲ τὸν ἥλιον ἔτι ῥᾳδίως ἀνέχομαι ὀξὺν καὶ φλογώδη ἐμπίπτοντα γυμνῇ τῇ κεφαλῇ. τὸν γὰρ πῖλόν μοι ἀφελεῖν οἴκοθεν ἔδοξεν, ὡς μὴ μόνος ἐν ὑμῖν ξενίζοιμι τῷ σχήματι. ἡ δὲ ὥρα τοῦ ἔτους ὅ τι περ τὸ πυρωδέστατόν ἐστι, τοῦ ἀστέρος ὃν ὑμεῖς κύνα φατὲ πάντα καταφλέγοντος καὶ τὸν ἀέρα ξηρὸν καὶ διακαῆ τιθέντος, ὅ τε ἥλιος κατὰ μεσημβρίαν ἤδη ὑπὲρ κεφαλῆς ἐπικείμενος φλογμὸν τοῦτον οὐ φορητὸν ἐπάγει τοῖς σώμασιν. ὥστε καὶ σοῦ θαυμάζω, ὅπως γηραιὸς ἤδη ἄνθρωπος οὔτε ἰδίεις πρὸς τὸ θάλπος ὥσπερ ἐγὼ οὔτε ὅλως ἐνοχλουμένῳ ἔοικας, οὐδὲ περιβλέπεις σύσκιόν τι ἔνθα ὑποδύσῃ, ἀλλὰ δέχῃ τὸν ἥλιον εὐμαρῶς.

benches over there, retreating to the shade so that those shouting at the wrestlers won't annoy us, especially since I, for it must be said, no longer bear easily the bright and blazing sun beating down on my naked head. I decided to leave my felt cap[14] at home so as not to be the only one among you dressed as a foreigner. It is the time of year, however, which is indeed the hottest with what you call the Dog Star burning up everything and making the air dry and scorching, and the midday sun now overhead presses down and brings this unbearable heat upon our bodies. So, I wonder at you, already an old man, how you neither sweat in the summer heat as I do, nor look like you are bothered at all. Nor are you looking around here for something shady to get under, but readily withstand the sun.

ΣΟΛΩΝ

Οἱ μάταιοι γὰρ οὗτοι πόνοι, ὦ Ἀνάχαρσι, καὶ αἱ συνεχεῖς ἐν τῷ πηλῷ κυβιστήσεις καὶ αἱ ὕπαιθροι ἐν τῇ ψάμμῳ ταλαιπωρίαι τοῦτο ἡμῖν τὸ ἀμυντήριον παρέχουσι πρὸς τὰς τοῦ ἡλίου βολάς, καὶ οὐκέτι πίλου δεόμεθα ὃς τὴν ἀκτῖνα κωλύσει καθικνεῖσθαι τῆς κεφαλῆς.

[17] Ἀπίωμεν δ᾽ οὖν. καὶ ὅπως μὴ καθάπερ νόμοις προσέξεις οἷς ἂν λέγω πρὸς σέ, ὡς ἐξ ἅπαντος πιστεύειν αὐτοῖς, ἀλλ᾽ ἔνθα ἄν σοι μὴ ὀρθῶς τι λέγεσθαι δοκῇ, ἀντιλέγειν εὐθὺς καὶ διευθύνειν τὸν λόγον. δυοῖν γὰρ θατέρου πάντως οὐκ ἂν ἁμάρτοιμεν, ἢ σὲ βεβαίως πεισθῆναι ἐκχέαντα ὁπόσα οἴει ἀντιλεκτέα εἶναι ἢ ἐμὲ ἀναδιδαχθῆναι ὡς οὐκ ὀρθῶς γιγνώσκω περὶ αὐτῶν. καὶ ἐν τούτῳ πᾶσα ἄν

Solon

These "pointless" exertions, Anacharsis, both the continual somersaults in the mud and the open-air hardships in the sand provide us a means of defense against the sun's beams. So we no longer need a felt cap to prevent the rays from coming down on our heads.

[17] But in any case, let us retreat. And do not look on the things I might say to you as if they were laws, trusting them in every way, but wherever it seems to you that something is not said correctly, contradict it immediately and set the argument straight. That way we would not fail to achieve one of two things: either you having been firmly persuaded after pouring out however many contradictions you think there are, or I having been taught that I do not comprehend these things correctly. And in this case, the

σοι ἡ πόλις ἡ Ἀθηναίων οὐκ ἄν φθάνοι χάριν ὁμολογοῦσα· ὅσα γὰρ ἂν ἐμὲ παιδεύσῃς καὶ μεταπείσῃς πρὸς τὸ βέλτιον, ἐκείνην τὰ μέγιστα ἔσῃ ὠφεληκώς. οὐδὲν γὰρ ἂν ἀποκρυψαίμην αὐτήν, ἀλλ᾽ εὐθὺς εἰς τὸ μέσον καταθήσω φέρων καὶ καταστὰς ἐν τῇ πνυκὶ ἐρῶ πρὸς ἅπαντας, "Ἄνδρες Ἀθηναῖοι, ἐγὼ μὲν ὑμῖν ἔγραψα τοὺς νόμους οἵους ᾤμην ὠφελιμωτάτους ἔσεσθαι τῇ πόλει, ὁ δὲ ξένος οὑτοσί"—δείξας σέ, ὦ Ἀνάχαρσι—"Σκύθης μέν ἐστι, σοφὸς δὲ ὢν μετεπαίδευσέ με καὶ ἄλλα βελτίω μαθήματα καὶ ἐπιτηδεύματα ἐδιδάξατο· ὥστε εὐεργέτης ὑμῶν ὁ ἀνὴρ ἀναγεγράφθω καὶ χαλκοῦν αὐτὸν ἀναστήσατε παρὰ τοὺς ἐπωνύμους <ἢ> ἐν πόλει παρὰ τὴν Ἀθηνᾶν."

whole city of the Athenians would not delay in acknowledging its gratitude to you; since to the extent that you educate me and persuade me to change for the better, you will have benefitted her in the greatest way. For I would hide nothing from her [the city], but immediately bringing it forward publicly, I will propose it while standing in the Pnyx.[15] I will say to everyone: "Men of Athens, for you I wrote the laws I thought would be most beneficial for the city, and this stranger"—having pointed to you, Anacharsis—"is a Scythian, yet being wise he has reeducated me and taught me other better doctrines and practices. So let the man be registered as your benefactor and set up a bronze [statue] of him beside the Eponymous Heroes or on the Acropolis beside the statue of Athena."[16]

καὶ εὖ ἴσθι ὡς οὐκ αἰσχυνεῖται ἡ Ἀθηναίων πόλις παρὰ βαρβάρου καὶ ξένου τὰ συμφέροντα ἐκμανθάνοντες.

ΑΝΑΧΑΡΣΙΣ

[18] Τοῦτ᾽ ἐκεῖνο ἦν ἄρα, ὃ ἐγὼ περὶ ὑμῶν ἤκουον τῶν Ἀθηναίων, ὡς εἴητε εἴρωνες ἐν τοῖς λόγοις. ἐπεὶ πόθεν ἂν ἐγὼ νομὰς καὶ πλάνης ἄνθρωπος, ἐφ᾽ ἁμάξης βεβιωκώς, ἄλλοτε ἄλλην γῆν ἀμείβων, πόλιν δὲ οὔτε οἰκήσας πώποτε οὔτε ἄλλοτε ἢ νῦν ἑωρακώς, περὶ πολιτείας διεξίοιμι καὶ διδάσκοιμι αὐτόχθονας ἄνδρας πόλιν ταύτην ἀρχαιοτάτην τοσούτοις ἤδη χρόνοις ἐν εὐνομίᾳ κατῳκηκότας, καὶ μαλιστα <σέ>, ὦ Σόλων, ᾧ τοῦτο ἐξ ἀρχῆς καὶ μάθημα, ὡς φασίν, ἐγένετο, ἐπίστασθαι ὅπως ἂν ἄριστα

Know well, [Anacharsis], that the city of the Athenians is not ashamed of having learned advantageous things from a non-Hellenic stranger.[17]

Anacharsis

[18] This is exactly the thing I heard about you Athenians, that you might be dissemblers in arguments. Since how can it be that I, a nomad and wandering person, having lived my life on a wagon, exchanging one land for another, never having inhabited a city nor even seen one other than now, might go through and teach men about government who have sprung from the earth[18] and inhabited in good order this most ancient of cities for so many years already—especially you, Solon, for whom, as they say, this has been a subject of study from the outset, namely, to know how a city would

πόλις οἰκοῖτο καὶ οἷστισιν νόμοις χρωμένη εὐδαιμονήσει; πλὴν ἀλλὰ καὶ τοῦτο ὡς νομοθέτῃ πειστέον σοι, καὶ ἀντερῶ ἤν τί μοι δοκῇ μὴ ὀρθῶς λέγεσθαι, ὡς βεβαιότερον μάθοιμι.

Καὶ ἰδοὺ γὰρ ἤδη ἐκφυγόντες τὸν ἥλιον ἐν τῷ συνηρεφεῖ ἐσμεν, καὶ καθέδρα μάλα ἡδεῖα καὶ εὔκαιρος ἐπὶ ψυχροῦ τοῦ λίθου. λέγε οὖν τὸν λόγον ἐξ ἀρχῆς καθ᾽ ὅ τι τοὺς νέους παραλαβόντες ἐκ παίδων εὐθὺς διαπονεῖτε, καὶ ὅπως ὑμῖν ἄριστοι ἄνδρες ἀποβαίνουσιν ἐκ τοῦ πηλοῦ καὶ τῶν ἀσκημάτων τούτων, καὶ τί ἡ κόνις καὶ τὰ κυβιστήματα συντελεῖ πρὸς ἀρετὴν αὐτοῖς. τοῦτο γὰρ δὴ μάλιστα ἐξ ἀρχῆς εὐθὺς ἐπόθουν ἀκοῦσαι· τὰ δ᾽ ἄλλα εἰς ὕστερον διδάξῃ με κατὰ καιρὸν ἕκαστον ἐν τῷ μέρει.

best be managed and which laws it would use to bring happiness? Nevertheless, I must obey you as a lawgiver in this, and I will contradict you if you seem to me to say something incorrectly, for in this way I would come to learn with more certainty.

And look, having now escaped the sun we are in the roofed-over area and there is a very pleasant and convenient place to sit on the cool stone.[19] So state your argument from the beginning. Now, after you take the young men into your care from childhood and immediately exert them strenuously, how do they turn out from the mud and these trainings to be your best men? And what do the dust and somersaults contribute toward their excellence? Indeed, straight from the outset I was anxious to hear this most of all, so teach me the rest later, each in turn at its appropriate time.

ἐκείνου μέντοι, ὦ Σόλων, μέμνησό μοι παρὰ τὴν ῥῆσιν, ὅτι πρὸς ἄνδρα βάρβαρον ἐρεῖς. λέγω δὲ ὡς μὴ περιπλέκῃς μηδὲ ἀπομηκύνῃς τοὺς λόγους· δέδια γὰρ μὴ ἐπιλανθάνωμαι τῶν πρώτων, ἥν τὰ μετὰ ταῦτα πολλὰ ἐπιρρέῃ.

ΣΟΛΩΝ

[19] Σὺ τοῦτο, ὦ Ἀνάχαρσι, ταμιεύσῃ ἄμεινον, ἔνθα ἄν σοι δοκῇ μὴ πάνυ σαφὴς ὁ λόγος εἶναι ἢ πόρρω ποι ἀποπλανᾶσθαι εἰκῇ ῥέων· ἐρήσῃ γὰρ μεταξὺ ὅ τι ἂν ἐθέλῃς καὶ διακόψεις αὐτοῦ τὸ μῆκος. ἢν μέντοι μὴ ἐξαγώνια μηδὲ πόρρω τοῦ σκοποῦ τὰ λεγόμενα ᾖ, κωλύσει οὐδέν, οἶμαι, εἰ καὶ μακρὰ λέγοιτο, ἐπεὶ καὶ τῇ βουλῇ τῇ ἐξ Ἀρείου πάγου, ἥπερ τὰς φονικὰς ἡμῖν δίκας δικάζει, πάτριον οὕτω ποιεῖν. ὁπόταν

But remember this especially in the course of your speech for me, Solon, that you will be speaking to a man who is non-Hellenic.[20] And I say this so that you do not complicate or draw out your arguments; for I fear that I might forget the first ones, should the ones afterwards flow on at great length.

Solon

[19] You will manage this better, Anacharsis. Wherever the argument seems to you not to be entirely clear or, when flowing randomly, to wander somewhere far off, then you interrupt to say whatever you wish and cut its length. However, if the things said are not out of bounds and not far from the mark, nothing hinders them, I think, from being spoken about for a long time, since even in the Council of the Areopagus, which judges murder cases for us, it is ancestral custom to

γὰρ ἀνελθοῦσα εἰς τὸν πάγον συγκαθέζηται φόνου ἢ τραύματος ἐκ προνοίας ἢ πυρκαϊᾶς δικάσοντες, ἀποδίδοται λόγος ἑκατέρῳ τῶν κρινομένων καὶ λέγουσιν ἐν τῷ μέρει ὁ μὲν διώκων ὁ δὲ φεύγων, ἢ αὐτοὶ ἢ ῥήτορας ἀναβιβάζονται τοὺς ἐροῦντας ὑπὲρ αὐτῶν. οἱ δὲ ἔστ᾽ ἂν μὲν περὶ τοῦ πράγματος λέγωσιν, ἀνέχεται ἡ βουλὴ καθ᾽ ἡσυχίαν ἀκούουσα· ἢν δέ τις ἢ φροίμιον εἴπῃ πρὸ τοῦ λόγου, ὡς εὐνουστέρους ἀπεργάσαιτο αὐτούς, ἢ οἶκτον ἢ δείνωσιν ἔξωθεν ἐπάγῃ τῷ πράγματι—οἷα πολλὰ ῥητόρων παῖδες ἐπὶ τοὺς δικαστὰς μηχανῶνται—παρελθὼν ὁ κῆρυξ κατεσιώπησεν εὐθύς, οὐκ ἐῶν ληρεῖν πρὸς τὴν βουλὴν καὶ περιπέττειν τὸ πρᾶγμα ἐν τοῖς

do so. For whenever, having gone up the hill, it [the Council] sits together in judgment of deliberate homicide or wounding or arson, the chance to speak is given to each of those being judged. The plaintiff and the defendant speak in turn, either in person or bringing forward rhetoricians to speak on their behalf. As long as they are speaking about the matter at hand, the Council bears it, listening quietly. But if, in order to make them more well-disposed, someone should give a preamble before the argument or bring in pity and exaggerated dread that is extraneous to the question—the sorts of things that rhetoricians contrive for the judges—then the herald having come forward imposes silence immediately. He does not allow talking nonsense before the Council and dressing up the matter at hand in words, thus the members of the Areopagus

λόγοις, ὡς γυμνὰ τὰ γεγενημένα οἱ Ἀρεοπαγῖται βλέποιεν.

Ὥστε καὶ σέ, ὦ Ἀνάχαρσι, Ἀρεοπαγίτην ἐν τῷ παρόντι ποιοῦμαι ἔγωγε, καὶ κατὰ τὸν τῆς βουλῆς μου νόμον ἄκουε, καὶ σιωπᾶν κέλευε, ἢν αἴσθῃ καταρρητορευόμενος· ἄχρι δ᾽ ἂν οἰκεῖα τῷ πράγματι λέγηται, ἐξέστω ἀπομηκύνειν. οὐδὲ γὰρ ὑφ᾽ ἡλίῳ ἔτι ποιησόμεθα τὴν συνουσίαν, ὡς ἄχθεσθαι εἰ ἀποτείνοιτο ἡ ῥῆσις, ἀλλὰ ἥ τε σκιὰ πυκνὴ καὶ ἡμεῖς σχολὴν ἄγομεν.

ΑΝΑΧΑΡΣΙΣ

Εὐγνώμονά σου ταῦτα, ὦ Σόλων, καὶ ἔγωγε ἤδη χάριν οὐ μικρὰν οἶδά σοι καὶ ἐπὶ τούτοις, ὅτι πάρεργον τοῦ λόγου καὶ τὰ ἐν Ἀρείῳ πάγῳ γιγνόμενα ἐδιδάξω με, θαυμάσια ὡς ἀληθῶς

perceive the events that took place *naked and unadorned.[21]

So, Anacharsis, for my part I hereby make you an Areopagite for the time being. In accordance with the law of my council, you listen and order me to be quiet if you feel overwhelmed by the rhetoric; but as long as the things said are related to our question, let it be possible to draw them out. After all, we will no longer be conversing under the sun so it is vexing if the speech were stretched out, but the shade is dense and we are at leisure.

Anacharsis

That is considerate of you, Solon, and I, for my part, am already not a little grateful to you for the things you taught me as a by-product of the discussion and those that take place in the Areopagus. These are truly

καὶ ἀγαθῶν βουλευτῶν ἔργα πρὸς ἀλήθειαν οἰσόντων τὴν ψῆφον. ἐπὶ τούτοις οὖν ἤδη λέγε, καὶ ὁ Ἀρεοπαγίτης ἐγὼ—τοῦτο γὰρ ἔθου με—κατὰ σχῆμα τῆς βουλῆς ἀκούσομαί σου.

ΣΟΛΩΝ

[20] Οὐκοῦν διὰ βραχέων προακοῦσαι χρή σε ἃ περὶ πόλεως καὶ πολιτῶν ἡμῖν δοκεῖ. πόλιν γὰρ ἡμεῖς οὐ τὰ οἰκοδομήματα ἡγούμεθα εἶναι, οἷον τείχη καὶ ἱερὰ καὶ νεωσοίκους, ἀλλὰ ταῦτα μὲν ὥσπερ σῶμά τι ἑδραῖον καὶ ἀκίνητον ὑπάρχειν εἰς ὑποδοχὴν καὶ ἀσφάλειαν τῶν πολιτευομένων, τὸ δὲ πᾶν κῦρος ἐν τοῖς πολίταις τιθέμεθα· τούτους γὰρ εἶναι τοὺς ἀναπληροῦντας καὶ διατάττοντας καὶ ἐπιτελοῦντας ἕκαστα καὶ φυλάττοντας, οἷόν τι ἐν ἡμῖν ἑκάστῳ ἐστὶν ἡ ψυχή.

wonderful and the work of good Council members who aim to cast their vote in accordance with truth. So speak now about these things, and I the Areopagite—for you made me this—will listen to you in the fashion of the Council.

Solon

[20] Then it is necessary for you to hear beforehand in a few words the things we believe about the city and citizens. We do not consider the city to be structures, such as walls and temples and docks, but those are, so to speak, a kind of stable and immovable body for the shelter and security of the governed. We place all authority in the citizens because they are the ones who fill it, arranging and prescribing and keeping watch over each matter; [they are] like the *mind is in each of us.

τοῦτο δὴ τοίνυν κατανοήσαντες ἐπιμελούμεθα μέν, ὡς ὁρᾷς, καὶ τοῦ σώματος τῆς πόλεως, κατακοσμοῦντες αὐτὸ ὡς κάλλιστον ἡμῖν εἴη, ἔνδοθέν τε οἰκοδομήμασιν κατεσκευασμένον καὶ ταῖς ἔκτοσθεν ταύταις περιβολαῖς εἰς τὸ ἀσφαλέστατον πεφραγμένον. μάλιστα δὲ καὶ ἐξ ἅπαντος τοῦτο προνοοῦμεν, ὅπως οἱ πολῖται ἀγαθοὶ μὲν τὰς ψυχάς, ἰσχυροὶ δὲ τὰ σώματα γίγνοιντο· τοὺς γὰρ τοιούτους σφίσι τε αὐτοῖς καλῶς χρήσεσθαι ἐν εἰρήνῃ συμπολιτευομένους καὶ ἐκ πολέμου σώσειν τὴν πόλιν καὶ ἐλευθέραν καὶ εὐδαίμονα διαφυλάξειν.

Τὴν μὲν δὴ πρώτην ἀνατροφὴν αὐτῶν μητράσι καὶ τίτθαις καὶ παιδαγωγοῖς ἐπιτρέπομεν ὑπὸ παιδείαις ἐλευθερίοις ἄγειν τε καὶ τρέφειν αὐτούς, ἐπειδὰν δὲ συνετοὶ ἤδη γίγνωνται τῶν καλῶς ἐχόντων, καὶ αἰδὼς καὶ ἐρύθημα καὶ φόβος καὶ ἐπιθυμία τῶν ἀρίστων

Having understood this, we also take care of the city's body, as you see, putting it in order so that it will be the most beautiful for us, equipped with structures on the inside and protected on the outside with these surrounding walls for the best security. But especially and most of all we provide for this: how the citizens might become good with respect to their minds and strong with respect to their bodies. As a consequence, such people will treat each other well in peace, engaged in the life of the city together, and will save it from war and preserve it free and happy.

So, we entrust their initial upbringing to their mothers and nurses and tutors to guide them by an *education for the free and to rear them. Then whenever they become aware of things that are good, and reverence and blushing [shame], and fear and a desire

ἀναφύηται αὐτοῖς, καὶ αὐτὰ ἤδη τὰ σώματα ἀξιόχρεα δοκῇ πρὸς τοὺς πόνους παγιώτερα γιγνόμενα καὶ πρὸς τὸ ἰσχυρότερον συνιστάμενα, τηνικαῦτα ἤδη παραλαβόντες αὐτοὺς διδάσκομεν, ἄλλα μὲν τῆς ψυχῆς μαθήματα καὶ γυμνάσια προτιθέντες, ἄλλως δὲ πρὸς τοὺς πόνους καὶ τὰ σώματα ἐθίζοντες.

οὐ γὰρ ἱκανὸν ἡμῖν ἔδοξε τὸ μόνον φῦναι ὡς ἔφυ ἕκαστος ἤτοι κατὰ τὸ σῶμα ἢ κατὰ τὴν ψυχήν, ἀλλὰ καὶ παιδεύσεως καὶ μαθημάτων ἐπ᾽ αὐτοὺς δεόμεθα, ὑφ᾽ ὧν τά τε εὐφυῶς διακείμενα βελτίω παρὰ πολὺ γίγνοιντο ἂν καὶ τὰ φαύλως ἔχοντα μετακοσμοῖτο πρὸς τὸ βέλτιον. καὶ τὸ παράδειγμα ἡμῖν παρὰ τῶν γεωργῶν, οἳ τὰ φυτὰ μέχρι μὲν πρόσγεια καὶ νήπιά ἐστι, σκέπουσιν καὶ περιφράττουσιν ὡς μὴ βλάπτοιντο ὑπὸ τῶν πνευμάτων, ἐπειδὰν δὲ ἤδη παχύνηται τὸ ἔρνος, τηνικαῦτα περιτέμνουσίν τε τὰ περιττὰ καὶ παραδόντες

for the most excellent things grows in them, and their bodies seem worthy for exertions, becoming more solid and strongly put together—at this time we take and teach them, but besides accustoming their bodies to exertions, we set up lessons and exercises of the mind.

To us it did not seem sufficient for each one to just grow naturally, either with respect to body or to mind; rather we need education and lessons for them through which what is naturally well-disposed becomes much better and things in poor condition are reordered for the better. And for us the example is from the farmers who, as long as the plants are young and close to the ground, cover and protect them all around so they are not harmed by the winds. But then whenever the shoots have thickened, at that time they prune the excess and, by

αὐτὰ τοῖς ἀνέμοις δονεῖν καὶ διασαλεύειν καρπιμώτερα ἐξεργάζονται.

[21] Τὴν μὲν τοίνυν ψυχὴν μουσικῇ τὸ πρῶτον καὶ ἀριθμητικῇ ἀναρριπίζομεν, καὶ γράμματα γράψασθαι καὶ τορῶς αὐτὰ ἐπιλέξασθαι διδάσκομεν· προϊοῦσιν δὲ ἤδη σοφῶν ἀνδρῶν γνώμας καὶ ἔργα παλαιὰ καὶ λόγους ὠφελίμους ἐν μέτροις κατακοσμήσαντες, ὡς μᾶλλον μνημονεύοιεν, ῥαψῳδοῦμεν αὐτοῖς. οἱ δὲ καὶ ἀκούοντες ἀριστείας τινὰς καὶ πράξεις ἀοιδίμους ὀρέγονται κατὰ μικρὸν καὶ πρὸς μίμησιν ἐπεγείρονται, ὡς καὶ αὐτοὶ ᾄδοιντο καὶ θαυμάζοιντο ὑπὸ τῶν ὕστερον. οἷα πολλὰ Ἡσίοδός τε ἡμῖν καὶ Ὅμηρος ἐποίησαν.

Ἐπειδὰν δὲ πλησιάζωσι πρὸς τὴν πολιτείαν καὶ δέῃ αὐτοὺς ἤδη μεταχειρίζεσθαι τὰ κοινά—καίτοι ἔξω τοῦ ἀγῶνος ἴσως ταῦτα· οὐ

giving them over to the winds to be shaken and buffeted, they render them more fruitful.

[21] Therefore, we rekindle the mind first with music and arithmetic, and we teach them to write their letters and to read them readily. And as they advance, we then recite to them maxims of wise men and ancient deeds and beneficial stories, having ordered these in meter so that they might better remember. And as they listen, little by little, they aspire toward certain feats of excellence and actions worthy of song and are roused to *imitation, so that they themselves might be sung about and wondered at by posterity. Both Hesiod and Homer composed many such things for us.

Whenever they enter government and it is then necessary for them to handle public affairs—but look, these things are perhaps

γὰρ ὅπως τὰς ψυχὰς αὐτῶν ἀσκοῦμεν ἐξ ἀρχῆς προὔκειτο εἰπεῖν, ἀλλὰ δι᾽ ὅ τι τοῖς τοιούτοις πόνοις καταγυμνάζειν αὐτοὺς ἀξιοῦμεν. ὥστε αὐτὸς ἐμαυτῷ σιωπᾶν προστάττω, οὐ περιμείνας τὸν κήρυκα οὐδὲ τὸν Ἀρεοπαγίτην σέ, ὃς ὑπ᾽ αἰδοῦς, οἶμαι, ἀνέχῃ ληροῦντα ἤδη τοσαῦτα ἔξω τοῦ πράγματος.

ΑΝΑΧΑΡΣΙΣ

Εἰπέ μοι, ὦ Σόλων, πρὸς δὲ δὴ τοὺς τὰ ἀναγκαιότατα μὴ λέγοντας ἐν Ἀρείῳ πάγῳ, ἀλλὰ ἀποσιωπῶντας, οὐδὲν τῇ βουλῇ πρόστιμον ἐπινενόηται;

ΣΟΛΩΝ

Τί τοῦτο ἤρου με; οὐδέπω γὰρ δῆλον.

out of bounds. How we train their minds from the beginning was not supposed to be the initial topic of discussion, but rather why we deem it worthy to exercise them so hard with such exertions. As a result, I order myself to be quiet—not waiting for the herald or for you, the Aeropagite, who might now, out of reverence, I think, be bearing my talking nonsense beyond the matter at hand.

Anacharsis

Tell me, Solon, for those who do not say what is most necessary in the Aeropagus, but keep silent, has no punishment been devised by the Council?

Solon

Why are you asking me this? So far it is not clear.

ΑΝΑΧΑΡΣΙΣ

Ὅτι τὰ κάλλιστα καὶ ἐμοὶ ἀκοῦσαι ἥδιστα παρείς, τὰ περὶ τῆς ψυχῆς, τὰ ἧττον ἀναγκαῖα λέγειν διανοῇ, γυμνάσια καὶ διαπονήσεις τῶν σωμάτων.

ΣΟΛΩΝ

Μέμνημαι γάρ, ὦ γενναῖε, τῶν ἀπ᾽ ἀρχῆς προρρήσεων καὶ ἀποπλανᾶν οὐ βούλομαι τὸν λόγον, μή σου ἐπιταράξῃ τὴν μνήμην ἐπιρρέων. πλὴν ἀλλὰ καὶ ταῦτα ἐρῶ διὰ βραχέων, ὡς οἷόν τε· τὸ γὰρ ἀκριβὲς τῆς περὶ αὐτῶν διασκέψεως ἑτέρου ἂν εἴη λόγου.

[22] Ῥυθμίζομεν οὖν τὰς γνώμας αὐτῶν νόμους τε τοὺς κοινοὺς ἐκδιδάσκοντες, οἳ δημοσίᾳ πᾶσι προκεινται ἀναγιγνώσκειν μεγάλοις γράμμασιν ἀναγεγραμμένοι, κελεύοντες ἅ τε χρὴ ποιεῖν καὶ ὧν ἀπέχεσθαι,

Anacharsis

Because you are neglecting the things most beautiful and pleasant for me to listen to, those concerning the mind, and you intend to speak about what is less necessary, exercises and strenuous exertions of bodies.

Solon

But I remember, noble one, the instructions set down at the beginning, and I do not wish to make the argument wander, lest by flowing on it confuse your memory. Nevertheless, I will speak also about these things as briefly as I can; for precision in examining them would be for another argument.

[22] As I was saying, we bring their judgments into proper measure by thoroughly teaching the laws shared in common. These are set out publicly, inscribed in large letters for everyone to read, commanding what

καὶ ἀγαθῶν ἀνδρῶν συνουσίαις, παρ᾽ ὧν λέγειν τὰ δέοντα ἐκμανθάνουσι καὶ πράττειν τὰ δίκαια καὶ ἐκ τοῦ ἴσου ἀλλήλοις συμπολιτεύεσθαι καὶ μὴ ἐφίεσθαι τῶν αἰσχρῶν καὶ ὀρέγεσθαι τῶν καλῶν, βίαιον δὲ μηδὲν ποιεῖν. οἱ δὲ ἄνδρες οὗτοι σοφισταὶ καὶ φιλόσοφοι πρὸς ἡμῶν ὀνομάζονται.

καὶ μέντοι καὶ εἰς τὸ θέατρον συνάγοντες αὐτοὺς δημοσίᾳ παιδεύομεν ὑπὸ κωμῳδίαις καὶ τραγῳδίαις ἀρετάς τε ἀνδρῶν παλαιῶν καὶ κακίας θεωμένους, ὡς τῶν μὲν ἀποτρέποιντο, ἐπ᾽ ἐκεῖνα δὲ σπεύδοιεν. τοῖς δέ γε κωμῳδοῖς καὶ λοιδορεῖσθαι καὶ ἀποσκώπτειν ἐφίεμεν εἰς τοὺς πολίτας οὓς ἂν αἰσχρὰ καὶ ἀνάξια τῆς πόλεως ἐπιτηδεύοντας αἴσθωνται, αὐτῶν τε

must be done and what avoided. Also, by conversing[22] with good men, they thoroughly learn what must be said and to do what is right, and to engage in the life of the city together in equality, and not to desire shameful things, but to aspire toward the good, and to do nothing by force. Among us, these men are called sophists and philosophers.[23]

In addition, we educate them publicly through comedies and tragedies, by bringing them together as spectators in the theater to view the excellences and vices of men of old. That way, they might turn away from the latter and be zealous about the former. Indeed, we permit the comic writers both to revile and to scoff at any citizens they might perceive to be practicing things shameful and unworthy of the city—not only for the sake of those men themselves, who become

ἐκείνων χάριν, ἀμείνους γὰρ οὕτω γίγνονται ὀνειδιζόμενοι, καὶ τῶν πολλῶν, ὡς φεύγοιεν τὸν ἐπὶ τοῖς ὁμοίοις ἔλεγχον.

ΑΝΑΧΑΡΣΙΣ

[23] Εἶδον, ὦ Σόλων, οὓς φὴς τοὺς τραγῳδοὺς καὶ κωμῳδούς, εἴ γε ἐκεῖνοί εἰσιν, ὑποδήματα μὲν βαρέα καὶ ὑψηλὰ ὑποδεδεμένοι, χρυσαῖς δὲ ταινίαις τὴν ἐσθῆτα πεποικιλμένοι, κράνη δὲ ἐπικείμενοι παγγέλοια κεχηνότα παμμέγεθες· αὐτοὶ δὲ ἔνδοθεν μεγάλα τε ἐκεκράγεσαν καὶ διέβαινον οὐκ οἶδ᾽ ὅπως ἀσφαλῶς ἐν τοῖς ὑποδήμασιν. Διονύσῳ δὲ οἶμαι τότε ἡ πόλις ἑώρταζεν. οἱ δὲ κωμῳδοὶ βραχύτεροι μὲν ἐκείνων καὶ πεζοὶ καὶ ἀνθρωπινώτεροι καὶ ἧττον ἐβόων, κράνη δὲ πολὺ γελοιότερα. καὶ τὸ θέατρον γοῦν ἅπαν ἐγέλα ἐπ᾽ αὐτοῖς·

better when thus reproached, but also for the many, so that they might shun scrutiny for similar things.

Anacharsis

[23] I saw the tragic and comic actors you speak of, Solon, if indeed these are the ones who, having tied on heavy elevated boots, festooned their clothing with golden ribbons and put on utterly ridiculous helmets with enormous gaping mouths.[24] They shouted loudly from within as they strode across [the stage]—who knows how without slipping in their boots. At the time the city was celebrating a festival for Dionysus, I believe. The comic actors, being on foot, were shorter than them [the tragic] and more human and they were shouting less, but their helmets were much more ridiculous. The spectators at least laughed at them,

ἐκείνων δὲ τῶν ὑψηλῶν σκυθρωποὶ ἅπαντες ἤκουον, οἰκτείροντες, οἶμαι, αὐτοὺς πέδας τηλικαύτας ἐπισυρομένους.

ΣΟΛΩΝ

Οὐκ ἐκείνους, ὦγαθέ, ᾤκτειρον, ἀλλὰ ποιητὴς ἴσως ἀρχαίαν τινὰ συμφορὰν ἐπεδείκνυτο τοῖς θεαταῖς καὶ ῥήσεις οἰκτρὰς ἐτραγῴδει πρὸς τὸ θέατρον ὑφ᾽ ὧν εἰς δάκρυα κατεσπῶντο οἱ ἀκούοντες. εἰκὸς δέ σε καὶ αὐλοῦντας ἑωρακέναι τινὰς τότε καὶ ἄλλους συνᾴδοντας ἐν κύκλῳ συνεστῶτας. οὐδ᾽ αὐτά, ὦ Ἀνάχαρσι, ἀχρεῖα ᾄσματα καὶ αὐλήματα.

Τούτοις δ᾽ οὖν ἅπασι καὶ τοῖς τοιούτοις παραθηγόμενοι τὰς ψυχὰς ἀμείνους ἡμῖν γίγνονται.

[24] Τὰ δὲ δὴ σώματα, ὅπερ μάλιστα ἐπόθεις ἀκοῦσαι, ὧδε καταγυμνάζομεν.

whereas they all listened gloomily to those elevated ones, pitying them, I think, for dragging along such great shackles.

Solon

It is not them [the actors] they were pitying, my good man, but perhaps a poet was displaying to the spectators some ancient misfortune and dramatizing pitiful speeches in the theater by which the listeners were reduced to tears. It is likely that you also saw some *aulos*-players at that time and others singing together standing in a circle.[25] Not even these songs and *aulos* music are useless, Anacharsis.

It is by these and all such things, then, that they [the youth] are sharpened with respect to their minds and become better for us.

[24] As for their bodies, which you were so anxious to hear about, we exercise them

ἀποδύσαντες αὐτά, ὡς ἔφην, οὐκέτι ἁπαλὰ καὶ τέλεον ἀσυμπαγῆ ὄντα, πρῶτον μὲν ἐθίζειν ἀξιοῦμεν πρὸς τὸν ἀέρα, συνοικειοῦντες αὐτὰ ταῖς ὥραις ἑκάσταις, ὡς μήτε θάλπος δυσχεραίνειν μήτε πρὸς κρύος ἀπαγορεύειν, ἔπειτα δὲ χρίομεν ἐλαίῳ καὶ καταμαλάττομεν, ὡς εὐτονώτερα γίγνοιτο· ἄτοπον γάρ, εἰ τὰ μὲν σκύτη νομίζομεν ὑπὸ τῷ ἐλαίῳ μαλαττόμενα δυσραγέστερα καὶ πολλῷ διαρκέστερα γίγνεσθαι νεκρά γε ἤδη ὄντα, τὸ δ᾽ ἔτι ζωῆς μετέχον σῶμα μὴ ἂν ἄμεινον ἡγοίμεθα ὑπὸ τοῦ ἐλαίου διατεθήσεσθαι.

Τοὐντεῦθεν ποικίλα τὰ γυμνάσια ἐπινοήσαντες καὶ διδασκάλους ἑκάστων ἐπιστήσαντες τὸν μέν τινα πυκτεύειν, τὸν δὲ παγκρατιάζειν διδάσκομεν, ὡς τούς τε πόνους καρτερεῖν ἐθίζοιντο καὶ ὁμόσε χωρεῖν ταῖς

hard in this way. Having stripped them, as I was saying, when they no longer are soft and completely undeveloped, we first deem it worthy to accustom them to the open air, familiarizing them with each of the seasons so as not to be bothered by heat nor to give in because of cold. Then we anoint them with olive oil and make them supple so that they might become more flexible; for it would be absurd if we recognized that leather, a thing actually dead, is harder to tear and becomes much more durable when softened by olive oil, yet we do not consider a body still partaking of life to be better conditioned by the olive oil.

From there, having invented various exercises and assigned teachers for each type, we teach one to box, another to do *pankration*, so that they might become accustomed to enduring exertions and to stand up to

πληγαις μηδὲ ἀποτρέποιντο δέει τῶν τραυμάτων. τοῦτο δὲ ἡμῖν δύο τὰ ὠφελιμώτατα ἐξεργάζεται ἐν αὐτοῖς, θυμοειδεῖς τε παρασκευάζον εἰς τοὺς κινδύνους καὶ τῶν σωμάτων ἀφειδεῖν καὶ προσέτι ἐρρῶσθαι καὶ καρτεροὺς εἶναι.

Ὅσοι δὲ αὐτῶν κάτω συννενευκότες παλαίουσιν, καταπίπτειν τε ἀσφαλῶς μανθάνουσι καὶ ἀνίστασθαι εὐμαρῶς καὶ ὠθισμοὺς καὶ περιπλοκὰς καὶ λυγισμοὺς καὶ ἄγχεσθαι δύνασθαι καὶ εἰς ὕψος ἀναβαστάσαι τὸν ἀντίπαλον, οὐκ ἀχρεῖα οὐδὲ οὗτοι ἐκμελετῶντες, ἀλλὰ ἓν μὲν τὸ πρῶτον καὶ μέγιστον ἀναμφιβόλως κτώμενοι· δυσπαθέστερα γὰρ καὶ καρτερώτερα τὰ σώματα γίγνονται αὐτοῖς διαπονούμενα.

ἕτερον δὲ οὐδὲ αὐτὸ μικρον· ἔμπειροι γὰρ δὴ ἐκ τούτου καθίστανται, εἴ ποτε ἀφίκοιντο

blows and to not turn away for fear of wounds. This renders in them two things most beneficial for us: it prepares them to be both spirited and unsparing of their bodies in the face of dangers, and on top of that, vigorous and capable of *endurance.

All those who wrestle with their heads lowered together learn both falling down safely and getting up readily, as well as pushing and clinching and twisting and being able to be choked, and to lift the opponent up high. And they are not practicing what is useless, but have acquired that one thing which is unambiguously the first and greatest: their bodies are in fact becoming impervious to pain and more capable of endurance from being strenuously exerted by them [their teachers].

And there is another thing that is not insignificant. As a result, they become

εἰς χρείαν τῶν μαθημάτων τούτων ἐν ὅπλοις· δῆλον γὰρ ὅτι καὶ πολεμίῳ ἀνδρὶ ὁ τοιοῦτος συμπλακεὶς καταρρίψει τε θᾶττον ὑποσκελίσας καὶ καταπεσὼν εἴσεται ὡς ῥᾷστα ἐξανίστασθαι. πάντα γὰρ ταῦτα, ὦ Ἀνάχαρσι, ἐπ᾽ ἐκεῖνον τὸν ἀγῶνα ποριζόμεθα τὸν ἐν τοῖς ὅπλοις καὶ ἡγούμεθα πολὺ ἀμείνοσι χρήσασθαι τοῖς οὕτως ἀσκηθεῖσιν, ἐπειδὰν πρότερον αὐτῶν γυμνὰ τὰ σώματα καταμαλάξαντες καὶ διαπονήσαντες ἐρρωμενέστερα καὶ ἀλκιμώτερα ἐξεργασώμεθα καὶ κοῦφα καὶ εὔπνοα καὶ τὰ αὐτὰ βαρέα τοῖς ἀνταγωνισταῖς.

[25] Ἐννοεῖς γάρ, οἶμαι, τὸ μετὰ τοῦτο, οἵους εἰκὸς σὺν ὅπλοις ἔσεσθαι τοὺς καὶ γυμνοὺς ἂν φόβον τοῖς δυσμενέσιν ἐμποιήσοντας, οὐ πολυσαρκίαν ἀργὸν καὶ λευκὴν ἢ ἀσαρκίαν μετὰ ὠχρότητος ἐπιδεικνυμένους οἷα

experienced from this should they ever come to need these lessons when they are in *arms; for it is clear that such a man, when entangled with an enemy, will throw him down more quickly after tripping him up, and after falling down will know how to get up readily. Thus, Anacharsis, all these things we supply for *that* competition, the one in arms. We consider men trained in this way much better to make use of, after having first made their naked bodies supple, and exerted them strenuously, and rendered them more vigorous and robust and light on their feet and aerobically fit and, by the same token, weighty for their antagonists.

[25] Therefore, you understand what follows, I think, the sort those [men] are likely to be with arms who, even naked, would create fear in those hostile to them. They would not display the idle and pasty obesity

γυναικῶν σώματα ὑπὸ σκιᾷ μεμαρασμένα, τρέμοντα ἱδρῶτί τε πολλῷ εὐθὺς ῥεόμενα καὶ ἀσθμαίνοντα ὑπὸ τῷ κράνει, καὶ μάλιστα ἢν καὶ ὁ ἥλιος ὥσπερ νῦν τὸ μεσημβρινὸν ἐπιφλέγῃ. οἷς τί ἄν τις χρήσαιτο διψῶσι καὶ τὸν κονιορτὸν οὐκ ἀνεχομένοις καὶ εἰ αἷμα ἴδοιεν, εὐθὺς ταραττομένοις καὶ προαποθνήσκουσι πρὶν ἐντὸς βέλους γενέσθαι καὶ εἰς χεῖρας ἐλθεῖν τοῖς πολεμίοις;

Οὗτοι δὲ ἡμῖν ὑπέρυθροι εἰς τὸ μελάντερον ὑπὸ τοῦ ἡλίου κεχρωσμένοι καὶ ἀρρενωποί, πολὺ τὸ ἔυψυχον καὶ θερμὸν καὶ ἀνδρῶδες ἐπιφαίνοντες, τοσαύτης εὐεξίας ἀπολάμποντες, οὔτε ῥικνοὶ καὶ κατεσκληκοτες οὔτε περιπληθεῖς εἰς βάρος, ἀλλὰ εἰς τὸ σύμμετρον περιγεγραμμένοι, τὸ μὲν ἀχρεῖον τῶν σαρκῶν καὶ περιττὸν τοῖς ἱδρῶσιν ἐξαναλωκότες, ὃ δὲ ἰσχὺν καὶ τόνον παρεῖχεν ἀμιγὲς τοῦ φαύλου περιλελειμμένον ἐρρωμένως φυλάττοντες.

or pallid scrawniness proper to women's bodies—withering in the shade, trembling, immediately streaming with much sweat, and gasping under their helmets—especially if the sun, just as now, is scorching at noon. For who could make use in any way of men thirsty and unable to bear the stirred-up dust; who when they see blood, are immediately thrown into disorder and are as good as dead before they are within spear-shot or come hand-to-hand with the enemies?

By contrast, ours are ruddy, having been colored darker by the sun, and with a manly aspect manifesting much spirit and *ardor and virility. Shining forth with so much fitness, they are neither shriveled and desiccated, nor bloated with weight, but symmetrically framed. They have used up what is useless and excessive of the flesh through sweating, while guarding robustly that

ὅπερ γὰρ δὴ οἱ λικμῶντες τὸν πυρόν, τοῦτο ἡμῖν καὶ τὰ γυμνάσια ἐργάζεται ἐν τοῖς σώμασι, τὴν μὲν ἄχνην καὶ τοὺς ἀθέρας ἀποφυσῶντα, καθαρὸν δὲ τὸν καρπὸν διευκρινοῦντα καὶ προσωρεύοντα.

[26] Καὶ διὰ τοῦτο ὑγιαίνειν τε ἀνάγκη καὶ ἐπὶ μήκιστον διαρκεῖν ἐν τοῖς καμάτοις· ὀψέ τε ἂν ἰδίειν ὁ τοιοῦτος ἄρξαιτο καὶ ὀλιγάκις ἂν ἀσθενῶν φανείη. ὥσπερ ἂν εἰ πῦρ τις φέρων ἅμα ἐμβάλοι εἰς πυρὸν αὐτὸν καὶ εἰς τὴν καλάμην αὐτοῦ καὶ εἰς τὴν ἄχνην—αὖθις γὰρ ἐπὶ τὸν λικμῶντα ἐπάνειμι—θᾶττον ἄν, οἶμαι, παρὰ πολὺ ἡ καλάμη ἀναφλεγείη, ὁ δὲ πυρὸς κατ᾽ ὀλίγον οὔτε φλογὸς μεγάλης ἀνισταμένης οὔτε ὑπὸ μιᾷ τῇ ὁρμῇ, ἀλλὰ κατὰ μικρὸν ὑποτυφόμενος χρόνῳ ὕστερον καὶ αὐτὸς ἂν κατακαυθείη.

which, left over and unmixed with worthlessness, provides strength and *tone. Indeed for us, exercises work on our bodies just as winnowers with wheat, the husks and chaff blown away, the clean grain separated and stored up.

[26] And for this reason they are necessarily healthy and persist in efforts for as long as possible; only after a long time would such a person start to sweat and seldom would they show signs of sickness. It is as if someone were to bring and simultaneously throw fire onto the wheat itself and onto its stalk and onto the husk, for again I return to the winnower. The stalk, I think, would flame up much more quickly, but the wheat, little by little with neither a great flame rising up nor with one burst, but smoldering bit by bit, at a later time would itself be completely burned up.

Οὐ τοίνυν οὐδὲ νόσος οὐδὲ κάματος εἰς τοιοῦτο σῶμα ἐμπεσόντα ῥᾳδίως ἐλέγξειεν ἂν οὐδ᾽ ἐπικρατήσειεν εὐμαρῶς· ἔνδοθέν τε γὰρ εὖ παρεσκεύασται αὐτῷ καὶ τὰ ἔξω μάλα καρτερῶς πέφρακται πρὸς αὐτά, ὡς μὴ παριέναι εἰς τὸ εἴσω, μηδὲ παραδέχεσθαι μήτε ἥλιον μήτε κρύος ἐπὶ λύμῃ τοῦ σώματος. πρός τε τὸ ἐνδιδὸν ἐν τοῖς πόνοις πολὺ τὸ θερμὸν τὸ ἔνδοθεν ἐπιρρέον, ἅτε ἐκ πολλοῦ προπαρεσκευασμένον καὶ εἰς τὴν ἀναγκαίαν χρείαν ἀποκείμενον, ἀναπληροῖ εὐθὺς ἐπάρδον τῇ ἀκμῇ καὶ ἀκαμάτους ἐπὶ πλεῖστον παρέχεται· τὸ γὰρ προπονῆσαι πολλὰ καὶ προκαμεῖν οὐκ ἀνάλωσιν τῆς ἰσχύος, ἀλλ᾽ ἐπίδοσιν ἐργάζεται, καὶ ἀναρριπιζομένη πλείων γίγνεται.

[27] Καὶ μὴν καὶ δρομικοὺς εἶναι ἀσκοῦμεν αὐτοὺς εἰς μῆκός τε διαρκεῖν ἐθίζοντες καὶ εἰς

Thus, neither illness nor weariness falling upon this sort of body would easily get the better of it or readily conquer it; since inside it is well-provided for by itself, and the outsides are very strongly barricaded against them so that they will not enter inside. Nor is the sun or cold admitted within to harm the body. During exertions there is much internal ardor that flows to any weak spot, insofar as it has been prepared long beforehand and reserved for use in case of need. It immediately fills them, irrigating them to their peak, and makes them indefatigable to the greatest extent. So much exertion and effort beforehand is therefore not a waste of strength but works to supplement it, since it becomes greater when rekindled.

[27] In fact we also train them to be runners, both accustoming them to persist for long distances and making them as nimble

τὸ ἐν βραχεῖ ὠκύτατον ἐπικουφίζοντες· καὶ ὁ δρόμος οὐ πρὸς τὸ στερρὸν καὶ ἀντίτυπον, ἀλλὰ ἐν ψάμμῳ βαθείᾳ, ἔνθα οὔτε βεβαίως ἀπερεῖσαι τὴν βάσιν οὔτε ἐπιστηρίξαι ῥᾴδιον ὑποσυρομένου πρὸς τὸ ὑπεῖκον τοῦ ποδός. ἀλλὰ καὶ ὑπεράλλεσθαι τάφρον, εἰ δέοι, ἢ εἴ τι ἄλλο ἐμπόδιον, καὶ πρὸς τοῦτο ἀσκοῦνται ἡμῖν, ἔτι καὶ μολυβδίδας χειροπληθεῖς ἐν ταῖν χεροῖν ἔχοντες. εἶτα περὶ ἀκοντίου βολῆς εἰς μῆκος ἁμιλλῶνται. εἶδες δὲ καὶ ἄλλο τι ἐν τῷ γυμνασίῳ χαλκοῦν περιφερές, ἀσπίδι μικρᾷ ἐοικὸς ὄχανον οὐκ ἐχούσῃ οὐδὲ τελαμῶνας, καὶ ἐπειράθης γε αὐτοῦ κειμένου ἐν τῷ μέσῳ καὶ ἐδόκει σοι βαρὺ καὶ δύσληπτον ὑπὸ λειότητος. ἐκεῖνο τοίνυν ἄνω τε ἀναρριπτοῦσιν εἰς τὸν ἀέρα καὶ εἰς τὸ πόρρω, φιλοτιμούμενοι ὅστις ἐπὶ μήκιστον ἐξέλθοι καὶ τοὺς ἄλλους ὑπερβάλοιτο·

and swift as possible for short distances. And the running is not on something solid and resistant, but in deep sand, where the footing is not firmly fixed nor easily supported, since one's foot is dragged down into the yielding ground. But they also jump over ditches if necessary or if there is any other obstacle. They are trained by us for this, even with as much lead weight as they can hold in their hands. Next, they contend in throwing the *javelin for distance. And you saw something else in the gymnasium, bronze and round like a small shield having neither a brace nor a strap, and you in fact tried it while it was lying there in the middle, and you thought it was heavy and hard to hold because of its smoothness. This they throw into the air and far off, contending in honor over who might reach the greatest distance and surpass the rest;

καὶ ὁ πόνος οὗτος ὤμους τε αὐτῶν κρατύνει καὶ τόνον τοῖς ἄκροις ἐντίθησιν.

[28] Ὁ πηλὸς δὲ καὶ ἡ κόνις, ἅπερ σοι γελοιότερα ἐξ ἀρχῆς ἔδοξεν, ἄκουσον, ὦ θαυμάσιε, ὅτου ἕνεκα ὑποβέβληται. πρῶτον μέν, ὡς μὴ ἐπὶ τὸ κραταιὸν ἡ πτῶσις αὐτοῖς γίγνοιτο, ἀλλ᾽ ἐπὶ τὸ μαλακὸν ἀσφαλῶς πίπτοιεν· ἔπειτα καὶ τὸν ὄλισθον ἀνάγκη πλείω γίγνεσθαι, ἱδρούντων ἐν τῷ πηλῷ, ὃ σὺ ταῖς ἐγχέλεσιν εἴκαζες, οὐκ ἀχρεῖον οὐδὲ γελοῖον ὄν, ἀλλὰ καὶ τοῦτο εἰς ἰσχὺν καὶ τόνον οὐκ ὀλίγα συντελεῖ, ὁπόταν οὕτως ἐχόντων ἀλλήλων ἀναγκάζωνται ἐγκρατῶς ἀντιλαμβάνεσθαι καὶ συνέχειν διολισθάνοντας· αἴρεσθαί τε ἐν πηλῷ ἱδρωκότα μετ᾽ ἐλαίου, ἐκπεσεῖν καὶ διαρρυῆναι τῶν χειρῶν σπουδάζοντα, μὴ μικρὸν εἶναι νόμιζε. καὶ ταῦτα πάντα, ὥσπερ ἔφην ἔμπροσθεν, εἰς τοὺς

and this exertion strengthens their shoulders and puts tone into their extremities.

[28] Now listen, wondrous one, to why the mud and the dust, which from the beginning seemed quite ridiculous to you, have been laid down. First, so that their falling would not be on something hard for them, but they would fall safely on some soft surface; and then, while sweating in the mud, their slipperiness, which you likened to eels, necessarily becomes greater. This is neither useless nor ridiculous, but it too assists with their strength and tone—whenever they are holding each other in this way they are forced to grip strongly and hold on while slippery. To lift someone in the mud, covered in sweat and olive oil and trying zealously to get away and slip through your hands—don't judge it insignificant. And all these things, as I said earlier, are also useful

πολέμους καὶ χρήσιμα, εἰ δέοι φίλον τρωθέντα ῥᾳδίως ἀράμενον ὑπεξενεγκεῖν ἢ καὶ πολέμιον συναρπάσαντα ἥκειν μετέωρον κομίζοντα. καὶ διὰ τοῦτο εἰς ὑπερβολὴν ἀσκοῦμεν, τὰ χαλεπώτερα προτιθέντες ὡς τὰ μικρότερα μακρῷ εὐκολώτερον φέροιεν.

[29] Τὴν μέντοι κόνιν ἐπὶ τὸ ἐναντίον χρησίμην οἰόμεθα εἶναι, ὡς μὴ διολισθάνοιεν συμπλεκόμενοι. ἐπειδὰν γὰρ ἐν τῷ πηλῷ ἀσκηθῶσιν συνέχειν τὸ διαδιδρᾶσκον ὑπὸ γλισχρότητος, ἐθίζονται ἐκφεύγειν αὐτοὶ ληφθέντες ἐκ τῶν χειρῶν, καὶ ταῦτα ἐν ἀφύκτῳ ἐχόμενοι. καὶ μὴν καὶ τὸν ἱδρῶτα συνέχειν δοκεῖ ἡ κόνις ἀθρόον ἐκχεόμενον ἐπιπαττομένη, καὶ ἐπὶ πολὺ διαρκεῖν ποιεῖ τὴν δύναμιν, καὶ κώλυμα γίγνεται μὴ βλάπτεσθαι ὑπὸ τῶν ἀνέμων ἀραιοῖς τότε καὶ ἀνεῳγόσιν τοῖς σώμασιν ἐμπιπτόντων.

in wars if it should be necessary to easily pick up and carry out a friend who has been wounded, or even an enemy, snatching and lifting him up and lugging him back. And for this reason we train *hyperbolically, adding more difficult things so that they tolerate the smaller ones far more easily.

[29] The dust, moreover, we think useful for the opposite [reason]: so that those entangled do not slip. For whenever they train in the mud to hold on to something that is getting away because of its slickness, they also become accustomed, when grasped themselves, to escape from another's hands, even while held in an inescapable hold. And indeed, the sprinkled on dust seems to hold back the flood of sweat and to make their power persist for a long time. Also, it becomes a defense against being harmed by the winds hitting their bodies when their pores

ἄλλως τε καὶ τὸν ῥύπον ἀποσμᾷ καὶ στιλπνότερον ποιεῖ τὸν ἄνδρα.

καὶ ἔγωγε ἡδέως ἂν παραστησάμενος πλησίον τῶν τε λευκῶν τινα ἐκείνων καὶ ὑπὸ σκιᾷ δεδιῃτημένων καὶ ὃν ἂν ἕλῃ τῶν ἐν τῷ Λυκείῳ γυμναζομένων, ἀποπλύνας τὴν κόνιν καὶ τὸν πηλόν, ἐροίμην ἄν σε ποτέρῳ ἂν ὅμοιος εὔξαιο γενέσθαι· οἶδα γὰρ ὡς αὐτίκα ἕλοιο ἂν ἐκ πρώτης προσόψεως, εἰ καὶ μὴ ἐπὶ τῶν ἔργων πειραθείης ἑκατέρου, συνεστηκὼς καὶ συγκεκροτημένος εἶναι μᾶλλον ἢ θρύπτεσθαι καὶ διαρρεῖν καὶ λευκὸς εἶναι ἀπορίᾳ καὶ φυγῇ εἰς τὰ εἴσω τοῦ αἵματος.

[30] Ταῦτ᾽ ἔστιν, ὦ Ἀνάχαρσι, ἃ τοὺς νέους ἡμεῖς ἀσκοῦμεν οἰόμενοι φύλακας ἡμῖν τῆς πόλεως ἀγαθοὺς γενέσθαι καὶ ἐν ἐλευθερίᾳ βιώσεσθαι δι᾽ αὐτούς, κρατοῦντες μὲν τῶν δυσμενῶν εἰ ἐπίοιεν, φοβεροὶ δὲ τοῖς

are open. In addition, it cleans off the filth and makes the man more glistening.

I, for my part, would gladly put one of those pallid[26] men who live in the shade side by side with whomever you might choose from those exercised in the Lyceum. Having cleaned off the dust and mud, I would ask you which of them you would pray to resemble. I know that right away from first sight, even if you had not tested what either could do, you would choose to be solid and disciplined rather than feeble and soft and pallid from lack of blood and its retreat to the insides.

[30] These are the things, Anacharsis, in which we train our young men, thinking that they become good guardians of our city. And because of them we will live in freedom, prevailing over those hostile to us if they attack, and be fearsome to our

περιοίκοις ὄντες, ὡς ὑποπτήσσειν τε καὶ ὑποτελεῖν ἡμῖν τοὺς πλείστους αὐτῶν. ἐν εἰρήνῃ τε αὖ πολὺ ἀμείνοσιν αὐτοῖς χρώμεθα περὶ μηδὲν τῶν αἰσχρῶν φιλοτιμουμένοις μηδ᾽ ὑπ᾽ ἀργίας εἰς ὕβριν τρεπομένοις, ἀλλὰ περὶ τὰ τοιαῦτα διατρίβουσιν καὶ ἀσχόλοις οὖσιν ἐν αὐτοῖς. καὶ ὅπερ ἔφην τὸ κοινὸν ἀγαθὸν καὶ τὴν ἄκραν πόλεως εὐδαιμονίαν, τοῦτ᾽ ἔστιν, ὁπόταν εἴς τε εἰρήνην καὶ εἰς πόλεμον τὰ ἄριστα παρεσκευασμένη φαίνοιτο ἡ νεότης περὶ τὰ κάλλιστα ἡμῖν σπουδάζοντες.

ΑΝΑΧΑΡΣΙΣ

[31] Οὐκοῦν, ὦ Σόλων, ἤν ποτε ὑμῖν ἐπίωσιν οἱ πολέμιοι, χρισάμενοι τῷ ἐλαίῳ καὶ κονισάμενοι πρόιτε καὶ αὐτοὶ πὺξ τὰς χεῖρας ἐπ᾽ αὐτοὺς προβεβλημένοι, κἀκεῖνοι δηλαδὴ

neighbors so that most of them will cower beneath us and pay us tribute.[27] In peacetime as well, we make much better use of them [our young men], who contend in honor over nothing shameful and do not turn towards violence out of idleness, but pass their time among themselves keeping busy with these kinds of things [exercises]. And again, what I was saying about the common good and the height of the city's well-being is this: once they have been prepared for peace and war in the best way, the youth would show themselves to be zealous about what for us is most beautiful.

Anacharsis

[31] So if enemies should ever attack you, Solon, then you yourselves, anointed with olive oil and dusted, will advance with clenched fists thrust out against them. And

ὑποπτήσσουσιν ὑμᾶς καὶ φεύγουσιν δεδιότες μὴ σφίσι κεχηνόσι πάσσητε τὴν ψάμμον εἰς τὸ στόμα ἢ περιπηδήσαντες, ὡς κατὰ νώτου γένησθε, περιπλέξητε αὐτοῖς τὰ σκέλη περὶ τὴν γαστέρα καὶ διάγχητε ὑπὸ τὸ κράνος ὑποβαλόντες τὸν πῆχυν. καὶ νὴ Δί᾽ οἱ μὲν τοξεύσουσι δῆλον ὅτι καὶ ἀκοντιοῦσιν, ὑμῶν δὲ ὥσπερ ἀνδριάντων οὐ καθίξεται τὰ βέλη κεχρωσμένων πρὸς τὸν ἥλιον καὶ πολὺ τὸ αἷμα πεπορισμένων. οὐ γὰρ καλάμη καὶ ἀθέρες ὑμεῖς ἐστε, ὡς τάχιστα ἐνδιδόναι πρὸς τὰς πληγάς, ἀλλὰ ὀψέ ποτε ἂν καὶ μόλις κατατεμνόμενοι βαθέσι τοῖς τραύμασιν αἷμα ὀλίγον ὑποδείξετε. [32] τοιαῦτα γὰρ φής, εἰ μὴ πάνυ παρήκουσα τοῦ παραδείγματος.

of course they will cower before you and flee, fearing that you might sprinkle sand into their mouths while they are agape. Or, having jumped around them to get on their back, you would clinch them around their belly with your legs, and you would strangle them, having put your forearm under their helmet. And they, by Zeus, will obviously be shooting arrows and throwing spears, yet the missiles will not stick in [you] who are just like statues tanned by the sun and supplied with plenty of blood. For you are not stalk and chaff, giving into blows as quickly as possible, but only after a long time and with difficulty, when you have been cut to pieces by deep wounds, will you show a little blood. [32] These are the kinds of things you are saying, unless I have completely misunderstood your example.

ἢ τὰς πανοπλίας ἐκείνας τότε ἀναλήψεσθε τὰς τῶν κωμῳδῶν τε καὶ τραγῳδῶν, καὶ ἢν προτεθῇ ὑμῖν ἔξοδος, ἐκεῖνα τὰ κράνη περιθήσεσθε τὰ κεχηνότα, ὡς φοβερώτεροι εἴητε τοῖς ἐναντίοις μορμολυττόμενοι αὐτούς, καὶ ὑποδήσεσθε τὰ ὑψηλὰ ἐκεῖνα δηλαδή· φεύγουσί τε γάρ, ἢν δέῃ, κοῦφα, καὶ ἢν διώκητε, ἄφυκτα τοῖς πολεμίοις ἔσται, ὑμῶν οὕτω μεγάλα διαβαινόντων ἐπ᾽ αὐτούς.

Ἀλλ᾽ ὅρα μὴ ταῦτα μὲν ὑμῖν τὰ κομψὰ λῆρος ᾖ καὶ παιδιὰ ἄλλως καὶ διατριβαὶ ἀργοῦσι καὶ ῥᾳθυμεῖν ἐθέλουσι τοῖς νεανίσκοις. εἰ δὲ βούλεσθε πάντως ἐλεύθεροι καὶ εὐδαίμονες εἶναι, ἄλλων ὑμῖν γυμνασίων δεήσει καὶ ἀσκήσεως ἀληθινῆς τῆς ἐν τοῖς ὅπλοις, καὶ ἡ ἅμιλλα οὐ πρὸς ἀλλήλους μετὰ παιδιᾶς, ἀλλὰ πρὸς τοὺς δυσμενεῖς ἔσται μετὰ κινδύνων μελετῶσι τὴν ἀρετήν. ὥστε ἀφέντας τὴν κόνιν καὶ τὸ ἔλαιον δίδασκε αὐτοὺς

Or maybe you will then take up those panoplies of the comic and tragic actors, and if an expedition is proposed to you, put on those gaping helmets so you would be more fearsome to adversaries and be boogeymen to them. And of course you will tie on those elevated things; for they will be light for fleeing in, if necessary, and make it impossible for enemies to escape if you are pursuing them with such great strides.

But beware lest these "refinements" of yours be nonsense and play and pastimes for the idle young wanting to take it easy. In any case, if you wish to be free and happy you will need other exercises and true training, the one in arms. And for those practicing to be excellent, the *contest will not be against one another in play but with dangers against those hostile to them.[28] So teach them, throwing away the dust and the olive oil, to

τοξεύειν καὶ ἀκοντίζειν μὴ κοῦφα διδοὺς τὰ ἀκόντια καὶ οἷα διαφέρεσθαι πρὸς τὸν ἄνεμον, ἀλλ᾽ ἔστω λόγχη βαρεῖα μετὰ συριγμοῦ ἑλιττομένη καὶ λίθος χειροπληθὴς καὶ σάγαρις καὶ γέρρον ἐν τῇ ἀριστερᾷ καὶ θώραξ καὶ κράνος.

[33] Ὡς δὲ νῦν ἔχετε, θεῶν τινος εὐμενείᾳ σώζεσθαί μοι δοκεῖτε, οἳ μηδέπω ἀπολώλατε ὑπό τινων ὀλίγων ψιλῶν ἐπιπεσόντων. ἰδού γέ τοι ἢν σπασάμενος τὸ μικρὸν τοῦτο ξιφίδιον τὸ παρὰ τὴν ζώνην μόνος ἐπεισπέσω τοῖς νέοις ὑμῶν ἅπασιν, αὐτοβοεὶ ἂν ἕλοιμι τὸ γυμνάσιον φυγόντων ἐκείνων καὶ οὐδενὸς ἀντιβλέπειν τῷ σιδήρῳ τολμῶντος, ἀλλὰ περὶ τοὺς ἀνδριάντας ἂν περιιστάμενοι καὶ περὶ τοὺς κίονας κατακρυπτόμενοι γέλωτα ἄν μοι παράσχοιεν δακρύοντες οἱ πολλοὶ καὶ τρέμοντες. καὶ τότ᾽ ἂν ἴδοις οὐκέτι ἐρυθριῶντας αὐτοὺς τὰ σώματα οἷοι νῦν εἰσιν,

shoot with the bow and to throw the spear, but not giving them light javelins that carry in the wind, rather let it be a heavy spear spinning with a hiss, and a stone that fills the hand, and an axe, and a wicker shield in the left hand, and a breastplate, and a helmet.

[33] In your current condition, you seem to me to be kept safe by the favor of one of the gods, given that you have not yet been destroyed by a few lightly-armed attackers. In fact, look, if I were to draw this small sword from my belt and attack all of your young men by myself, I would capture the gymnasium with a mere shout—not one daring to face my iron weapon as they flee. Rather, turning to escape among the statues and hiding behind the columns, most of them crying and trembling, they would provide me with laughter. At that time you would no longer see them ruddy in body as

ἀλλὰ ὠχροὶ ἅπαντες αὐτίκα γένοιντ᾽ ἂν ὑπὸ τοῦ δέους μεταβαφέντες. οὕτως ὑμᾶς ἡ εἰρήνη διατέθεικε βαθεῖα οὖσα, ὡς μὴ ἂν ῥᾳδίως ἀνασχέσθαι λόφον ἕνα κράνους πολεμίου ἰδόντας.

ΣΟΛΩΝ

[34] Οὐ ταῦτα ἔφασαν, ὦ Ἀνάχαρσι, Θρᾳκῶν τε ὅσοι μετ᾽ Εὐμόλπου ἐφ᾽ ἡμᾶς ἐστράτευσαν καὶ αἱ γυναῖκες ὑμῶν αἱ μετὰ Ἱππολύτης ἐλάσασαι ἐπὶ τὴν πόλιν οὐδὲ οἱ ἄλλοι ὅσοι ἡμῶν ἐν ὅπλοις ἐπειράθησαν. ἡμεῖς γάρ, ὦ μακάριε, οὐκ ἐπείπερ οὕτω γυμνὰ τὰ σώματα ἐκπονοῦμεν τῶν νέων, διὰ τοῦτο καὶ ἄνοπλα ἐξάγομεν ἐπὶ τοὺς κινδύνους, ἀλλ᾽ ἐπειδὰν καθ᾽ αὑτοὺς ἄριστοι γένωνται, ἀσκοῦνται τὸ μετὰ τοῦτο σὺν τοῖς ὅπλοις, καὶ πολὺ ἄμεινον χρήσαιντ᾽ ἂν αὐτοῖς οὕτω διακείμενοι.

they are now, but they would all become pale right away, dyed by fear. The present peace, being so secure, has put you in such a state that you couldn't easily bear seeing the crest of a single enemy helmet.

Solon

[34] The Thracians who campaigned against us with Eumolpus did not say these things, Anacharsis, nor did your women who marched against the city with Hippolyta,[29] nor all the rest of those who tested us in arms. For even though, blessed one, we exert the bodies of our young men naked in this way, we do not for this reason also lead them out unarmed against dangers. Rather, whenever they become best in their own right, after this they train with arms and, once conditioned in this way, make far better use of them.

ΑΝΑΧΑΡΣΙΣ

Καὶ ποῦ τοῦτο ὑμῖν ἐστι τὸ γυμνάσιον τὸ ἐν τοῖς ὅπλοις; οὐ γὰρ εἶδον ἔγωγε ἐν τῇ πόλει τοιοῦτον οὐδέν, ἅπασαν αὐτὴν ἐν κύκλῳ περιελθών.

ΣΟΛΩΝ

Ἀλλὰ ἴδοις ἄν, ὦ Ἀνάχαρσι, ἐπὶ πλέον ἡμῖν συνδιατρίψας, καὶ ὅπλα ἑκάστῳ μάλα πολλά, οἷς χρώμεθα ὁπόταν ἀναγκαῖον ᾖ, καὶ λόφους καὶ φάλαρα καὶ ἵππους, καὶ ἱππέας σχεδὸν τὸ τέταρτον τῶν πολιτῶν. τὸ μέντοι ὁπλοφορεῖν ἀεὶ καὶ ἀκινάκην παρεζῶσθαι περιττὸν ἐν εἰρήνῃ οἰόμεθα εἶναι, καὶ πρόστιμόν γ' ἔστιν, ὅστις ἐν ἄστει σιδηροφοροίη μηδὲν δέον ἢ ὅπλα ἐξενέγκοι εἰς τὸ δημόσιον.

Anacharsis

And where is this gymnasium of yours, the one for [training] in arms? For I myself have not seen any such thing in the city, though I have circled all of it.

Solon

But after passing more time with us, Anacharsis, you would see that each of us possesses very many arms, which we make use of whenever necessary, and also crests and bosses and horses since almost a quarter of the citizens are horsemen. To always carry arms, however, and to strap on a Scythian dagger in peacetime we think is excessive. In fact, there is a punishment for anyone who unnecessarily carries iron weapons within the city or carries arms out into a public place.

ὑμεῖς δὲ συγγνωστοὶ ἐν ὅπλοις ἀεὶ βιοῦντες· τό τε γὰρ ἐν ἀφράκτῳ οἰκεῖν ῥᾴδιον εἰς ἐπιβουλήν, καὶ οἱ πόλεμοι μάλα πολλοί, καὶ ἄδηλον ὁπότε τις ἐπιστὰς κοιμώμενον κατασπάσας ἀπὸ τῆς ἁμάξης φονεύσειεν· ἥ τε πρὸς ἀλλήλους ἀπιστία, καὶ μὴ ἐν νόμῳ συμπολιτευομένων, ἀναγκαῖον ἀεὶ τὸν σίδηρον ποιεῖ, ὡς πλησίον εἶναι ἀμυνοῦντα, εἴ τις βιάζοιτο.

ΑΝΑΧΑΡΣΙΣ

[35] Εἶτα, ὦ Σόλων, σιδηροφορεῖν μὲν οὐδενὸς ἀναγκαίου ἕνεκα περιττὸν ὑμῖν δοκεῖ, καὶ τῶν ὅπλων φείδεσθε, ὡς μὴ διὰ χειρὸς ὄντα φθείροιτο, ἀλλὰ φυλάττετε ἀποκείμενα ὡς χρησόμενοι τότε, τῆς χρείας

You [Scythians], however, are excused for always living in arms; for inhabiting an unfortified place makes ambush easy, and your wars are very many. It is uncertain whenever someone, coming by surprise on one sleeping, might drag him out of his wagon and kill him. Both your mistrust of one another and failure to engage in the life of the city together under the rule of law make it imperative always to have weapons at the ready, so that you can defend yourselves against any threat of force.

Anacharsis

[35] And so it seems excessive to you to carry iron weapons when there is no necessity, Solon, and you are sparing of your arms lest they be worn out by being handled, guarding them instead in reserve so that you can use them when a time of need comes

ἐπιστάσης· τὰ δὲ σώματα τῶν νέων οὐδενὸς δεινοῦ ἐπείγοντος καταπονεῖτε παίοντες καὶ ὑπὸ τῶν ἱδρώτων καταναλίσκοντες, οὐ ταμιευόμενοι πρὸς τὸ ἀναγκαῖον τὰς ἀλκὰς αὐτῶν, ἀλλ' εἰκῆ ἐν τῷ πηλῷ καὶ τῇ κόνει ἐκχέοντες;

ΣΟΛΩΝ

Ἔοικας, ὦ Ἀνάχαρσι, τοιόνδε τι δυνάμεως πέρι ἐννοεῖν, ὡς οἴνῳ ἢ ὕδατι ἢ ἄλλῳ τῶν ὑγρῶν ὁμοίαν αὐτὴν οὖσαν. δέδιας οὖν μὴ ὥσπερ ἐξ ἀγγείου κεραμεοῦ λάθῃ διαρρυεῖσα ἐν τοῖς πόνοις κᾆτα ἡμῖν κενὸν καὶ ξηρὸν οἴχηται τὸ σῶμα καταλιποῦσα ὑπὸ μηδενὸς ἔνδοθεν ἀναπληρούμενον. τὸ δὲ οὐχ οὕτως ἔχει σοι, ἀλλὰ ὅσῳ τις ἂν αὐτὴν ἐξαντλῇ τοῖς πόνοις, τοσῷδε μᾶλλον ἐπιρρεῖ κατὰ τὸν περὶ

upon you. And yet, even when nothing terrible is pressing, you wear down your young men's bodies hitting and completely using them up by sweating, not saving up their prowess for when it is needed, but pouring it out randomly in mud and dust?

Solon

Anacharsis, it looks like you have something of this sort in mind about power, that it is similar to wine or water or another of the liquids. For you are afraid that, just as from an earthen vessel, it might leak out unnoticed during their exertions and then vanish, having left their bodies behind empty and dry, with nothing to refill them from within. But it is not as you have it. Rather, as much as someone drains it [power] away in exertions, so much the more it [power] flows in—as in the tale about the Hydra, if you've

τῆς Ὕδρας μῦθον, εἴ τινα ἤκουσας, ὡς ἀντὶ μιᾶς κεφαλῆς τμηθείσης δύ᾽ ἀεὶ ἄλλαι ἀνεφύοντο.

ἢν δὲ ἀγύμναστος ἐξ ἀρχῆς καὶ ἄτονος ᾖ μηδὲ διαρκῆ τὴν ὕλην ἔχῃ ὑποβεβλημένην, τότε ὑπὸ τῶν καμάτων βλάπτοιτο ἂν καὶ καταμαραίνοιτο, οἷόν τι ἐπὶ πυρὸς καὶ λύχνου γίγνεται. ὑπὸ γὰρ τῷ αὐτῷ φυσήματι τὸ μὲν πῦρ ἀνακαύσειας ἂν καὶ μεῖζον ἐν βραχεῖ ποιήσειας παραθήγων τῷ πνεύματι, καὶ τὸ τοῦ λύχνου φῶς ἀποσβέσειας οὐκ ἔχον ἀποχρῶσαν τῆς ὕλης τὴν χορηγίαν, ὡς διαρκῆ εἶναι πρὸς τὸ ἀντιπνέον· οὐ γὰρ ἀπ᾽ ἰσχυρᾶς, οἶμαι, τῆς ῥίζης ἀνεφύετο.

ΑΝΑΧΑΡΣΙΣ

[36] Ταυτὶ μέν, ὦ Σόλων, οὐ πάνυ συνίημι· λεπτότερα γὰρ ἢ κατ᾽ ἐμὲ εἴρηκας, ἀκριβοῦς

heard the one, that when one of her heads is cut off, two others always spring up instead.

However, if someone from the outset were neither exercising, nor toned, and had no sufficient store of fuel laid up, then he would be harmed by his efforts and would completely wither away. This happens, for example, with fire and a lamp, for with the same amount of blowing you would either light up the fire and quickly make it greater, intensifying it with breath. Or you could extinguish the light of the lamp if it lacks the abundance of fuel to persist in the face of what is blowing against it because, I think, it was not growing from a strong source.

Anacharsis

[36] I do not completely understand this, Solon; for you have said things that are more

τινος φροντίδος καὶ διανοίας ὀξὺ δεδορκυίας δεόμενα. ἐκεῖνο δέ μοι πάντως εἰπέ, τίνος ἕνεκα οὐχὶ καὶ ἐν τοῖς ἀγῶσι τῷ Ὀλυμπίασι καὶ Ἰσθμοῖ καὶ Πυθοῖ καὶ τοῖς ἄλλοις, ὁπότε πολλοί, ὡς φής, συνίασιν ὀψόμενοι τοὺς νέους ἀγωνιζομένους, οὐδέποτε ἐν ὅπλοις ποιεῖσθε τὴν ἅμιλλαν, ἀλλὰ γυμνοὺς εἰς τὸ μέσον παραγαγόντες λακτιζομένους καὶ παιομένους ἐπιδείκνυτε καὶ νικήσασι μῆλα καὶ κότινον δίδοτε; ἄξιον γὰρ εἰδέναι τοῦτό γε, οὗτινος ἕνεκα οὕτω ποιεῖτε.

ΣΟΛΩΝ

Ἡγούμεθα γάρ, ὦ Ἀνάχαρσι, τὴν εἰς τὰ γυμνάσια προθυμίαν οὕτως ἂν πλείω ἐγγενέσθαι αὐτοῖς, εἰ τοὺς ἀριστεύοντας ἐν τούτοις ἴδοιεν τιμωμένους καὶ ἀνακηρυττομένους ἐν μέσοις τοῖς Ἕλλησι. Καὶ διὰ τοῦτο ὡς εἰς τοσούτους ἀποδυσόμενοι

subtle than I am used to, requiring a certain precision of thought and a sharp-sighted intellect. But in any case, tell me this, why at the Olympian and Isthmian and Pythian competitions and all the rest, whenever many assemble in order to watch the young men competing, as you say, you never have them contest in arms but, bringing them forward naked, you display them kicking and hitting, and to the victorious you give apples and an olive wreath? It is worth knowing this at least: to what end[30] you are doing so.

Solon

It is because we consider, Anacharsis, that their eagerness for exercises will thus increase if they see those excelling in these things honored and proclaimed by heralds amidst the Hellenes. And for this reason, in order to undress before so many, they take

εὐεξίας τε ἐπιμελοῦνται, ὡς μὴ αἰσχύνοιντο γυμνωθέντες, καὶ ἀξιονικότατον ἕκαστος αὑτὸν ἀπεργάζεται.

Καὶ τὰ ἆθλα, ὥσπερ ἔμπροσθεν εἶπον, οὐ μικρά, ὁ ἔπαινος ὁ παρὰ τῶν θεατῶν καὶ τὸ ἐπισημότατον γενέσθαι καὶ δείκνυσθαι τῷ δακτύλῳ ἄριστον εἶναι τῶν καθ᾽ αὑτὸν δοκοῦντα. Τοιγάρτοι πολλοὶ τῶν θεατῶν, οἷς καθ᾽ ἡλικίαν ἔτι ἄσκησις, ἀπίασιν οὐ μετρίως ἐκ τῶν τοιούτων ἀρετῆς καὶ πόνων ἐρασθέντες.

ὡς εἴ γέ τις, ὦ Ἀνάχαρσι, τὸν τῆς εὐκλείας ἔρωτα ἐκβάλοι ἐκ τοῦ βίου, τί ἂν ἔτι ἀγαθὸν ἡμῖν γένοιτο, ἢ τίς ἄν τι λαμπρὸν ἐργάσασθαι ἐπιθυμήσειεν; νῦν δὲ καὶ ἀπὸ τούτων εἰκάζειν παρέχοιεν ἄν σοι, ὁποῖοι ἐν πολέμοις ὑπὲρ πατρίδος καὶ παίδων καὶ γυναικῶν καὶ ἱερῶν

care of their fitness so they are not ashamed when naked, and each makes himself most worthy of victory.

And the prizes, as I said earlier, are not insignificant, namely, the praise of the spectators, and becoming the most distinguished, and having fingers pointed at oneself for being thought the best of one's cohort. And indeed, many of the spectators who are still at the age for training go away from such events having fallen immoderately in love with excellence and exertions.

So, in fact, Anacharsis, if someone were to expel the love of glory from life, what good would we ever obtain, or who would desire to achieve anything brilliant? Now, however, you can imagine even from these things what sort [of men] they would become in wars, armed on behalf of their fatherland and their children and their wives

γένοιντ᾽ ἂν ὅπλα ἔχοντες οἱ κοτίνου πέρι καὶ μήλων γυμνοὶ τοσαύτην προθυμίαν εἰς τὸ νικᾶν εἰσφερόμενοι.

[37] Καίτοι τί ἂν πάθοις, εἰ θεάσαιο καὶ ὀρτύγων καὶ ἀλεκτρυόνων ἀγῶνας παρ᾽ ἡμῖν καὶ σπουδὴν ἐπὶ τούτοις οὐ μικράν; ἢ γελάσῃ δῆλον ὅτι, καὶ μάλιστα ἢν μάθῃς ὡς ὑπὸ νόμῳ αὐτὸ δρῶμεν καὶ προστέτακται πᾶσι τοῖς ἐν ἡλικίᾳ παρεῖναι καὶ ὁρᾶν τὰ ὄρνεα διαπυκτεύοντα μέχρι τῆς ἐσχάτης ἀπαγορεύσεως; ἀλλ᾽ οὐδὲ τοῦτο γελοῖον· ὑποδύεται γάρ τις ἠρέμα ταῖς ψυχαῖς ὁρμὴ εἰς τοὺς κινδύνους, ὡς μὴ ἀγεννέστεροι καὶ ἀτολμότεροι φαίνοιντο τῶν ἀλεκτρυόνων μηδὲ προαπαγορεύοιεν ὑπὸ τραυμάτων ἢ καμάτου ἤ του ἄλλου δυσχεροῦς.

Τὸ δὲ δὴ ἐν ὅπλοις πειρᾶσθαι αὐτῶν καὶ ὁρᾶν τιτρωσκομένους—ἄπαγε· θηριῶδες γὰρ καὶ δεινῶς σκαιὸν καὶ προσέτι γε ἀλυσιτελὲς

and their temples, those who [competing] naked for wild olive and apples brought in such great eagerness for victory.

[37] And what would your reaction be if you saw the quail fights and cockfights among us and our not insignificant zeal for them? Or is it clear that you would laugh, especially if you should learn that we do this by law and that it is mandated for all those of age to be present and to watch the birds fighting to the furthest possible limit of exhaustion?[31] But neither is this laughable; for a certain impulse toward dangers quietly steals into their minds, so that they neither show themselves more ignoble and less daring than the cocks nor give in because of wounds or fatigue or any other difficulty.

But as for testing [men] in arms and seeing them wounded—no thanks; for that is animalistic and terribly ill-omened. Indeed, on

ἀποσφάττειν τοὺς ἀρίστους καὶ οἷς ἄν τις ἄμεινον χρήσαιτο κατὰ τῶν δυσμενῶν.

[38] Ἐπεὶ δὲ φής, ὦ Ἀνάχαρσι, καὶ τὴν ἄλλην Ἑλλάδα ἐπελεύσεσθαι, μέμνησο ἤν ποτε καὶ εἰς Λακεδαίμονα ἔλθῃς, μὴ καταγελάσαι μηδὲ ἐκείνων μηδὲ οἴεσθαι μάτην πονεῖν αὐτούς, ὁπόταν ἢ σφαίρας πέρι ἐν τῷ θεάτρῳ συμπεσόντες παίωσιν ἀλλήλους ἢ εἰς χωρίον εἰσελθόντες ὕδατι περιγεγραμμένον, εἰς φάλαγγα διαστάντες, τὰ πολεμίων ἀλλήλους ἐργάζωνται γυμνοὶ καὶ αὐτοί, ἄχρις ἂν ἐκβάλωσι τοῦ περιγράμματος τὸ ἕτερον σύνταγμα οἱ ἕτεροι, τοὺς κατὰ Λυκοῦργον οἱ καθ' Ἡρακλέα ἢ ἔμπαλιν, συνωθοῦντες εἰς τὸ ὕδωρ· τὸ γὰρ ἀπὸ τούτου εἰρήνη λοιπὸν καὶ οὐδεὶς ἂν ἔτι παίσειε. μάλιστα δὲ ἢν ὁρᾷς μαστιγουμένους αὐτοὺς ἐπὶ τῷ βωμῷ καὶ αἵματι ῥεομένους, πατέρας δὲ καὶ μητέρας παρεστώσας οὐχ ὅπως

top of that, it is not profitable to slaughter the best, whom one might make better use of against those hostile to us.

[38] Since you say that you are going to visit the rest of Greece, Anacharsis, remember if you ever go to Sparta, do not mock them either. Do not think that they exert themselves pointlessly whenever they are hitting one another after clashing around a ball in the theater, or going into a space bounded by water, separated into phalanxes—they too naked—and treating one another as enemies until one group drives the other contingent out of the bounded area, either the Heracleans pushing the *Lycurgians into the water or vice-versa, for after this peace remains and no one hits any longer.[32]

[Do not mock them] especially if you see them whipped on the altar and streaming with blood, their fathers and mothers

ἀνιωμένας ἐπὶ τοῖς γιγνομένοις ἀλλὰ καὶ ἀπειλούσας, εἰ μὴ ἀντέχοιεν πρὸς τὰς πληγάς, καὶ ἱκετευούσας ἐπὶ μήκιστον διαρκέσαι πρὸς τὸν πόνον καὶ ἐγκαρτερῆσαι τοῖς δεινοῖς. πολλοὶ γοῦν καὶ ἐναπέθανον τῷ ἀγῶνι μὴ ἀξιώσαντες ἀπαγορεῦσαι ζῶντες ἔτι ἐν ὀφθαλμοῖς τῶν οἰκείων μηδὲ εἶξαι τοῖς σώμασιν· ὧν καὶ τοὺς ἀνδριάντας ὄψει τιμωμένους δημοσίᾳ ὑπὸ τῆς Σπάρτης ἀνασταθέντας.

Ὅταν τοίνυν ὁρᾷς κἀκεῖνα, μήτε μαίνεσθαι ὑπολάβῃς αὐτοὺς μήτε εἴπῃς ὡς οὐδεμιᾶς ἕνεκα αἰτίας ἀναγκαίας ταλαιπωροῦσι, μήτε τυράννου βιαζομένου μήτε πολεμίων διατιθέντων. εἴποι γὰρ ἄν σοι καὶ ὑπὲρ ἐκείνων Λυκοῦργος ὁ νομοθέτης αὐτῶν πολλὰ τὰ εὔλογα καὶ ἃ συνιδὼν κολάζει αὐτούς, οὐκ ἐχθρὸς ὢν οὐδὲ ὑπὸ μίσους αὐτὸ δρῶν οὐδὲ τὴν νεολαίαν

standing by, not distressed by what is taking place but even threatening them if they do not bear up against the lashes and praying that they resist the pain as long as possible and endure the terrors. Many, in fact, have died in the competitions, not deeming it worthy while still alive to give in before the eyes of their family nor to yield physically; you will even see statues of them set up by Sparta being honored publicly.[33]

Whenever, then, you see these things, do not take them to be mad or say that they are undergoing hardships for no necessary reason, with neither a tyrant coercing nor enemies lined up against them. For Lycurgus, the lawgiver, might tell you much that is reasonable in favor of these things and his grounds for punishing them despite not being their enemy. Neither is he doing it from hatred nor randomly squandering the

τῆς πόλεως εἰκῆ παραναλίσκων, ἀλλὰ καρτερικωτάτους καὶ παντὸς δεινοῦ κρείττονας ἀξιῶν εἶναι τοὺς σώσειν μέλλοντας τὴν πατρίδα.

καίτοι κἂν μὴ ὁ Λυκοῦργος εἴπῃ, ἐννοεῖς, οἶμαι, καὶ αὐτὸς ὡς οὐκ ἄν ποτε ληφθεὶς ὁ τοιοῦτος ἐν πολέμῳ ἀπόρρητόν τι ἐξείποι τῆς Σπάρτης αἰκιζομένων τῶν ἐχθρῶν, ἀλλὰ καταγελῶν αὐτῶν μαστιγοῖτο ἂν ἁμιλλώμενος πρὸς τὸν παίοντα, ὁπότερος ἀπαγορεύσειεν.

ΑΝΑΧΑΡΣΙΣ

[39] Ὁ Λυκοῦργος δὲ καὶ αὐτός, ὦ Σόλων, ἐμαστιγοῦτο ἐφ᾽ ἡλικίας, ἢ ἐκπρόθεσμος ὢν ἤδη τοῦ ἀγῶνος ἀσφαλῶς τὰ τοιαῦτα ἐνεανιεύσατο;

youth of the city, but because he deems it worthy that those who are to save their fatherland be the most capable of endurance and stronger in the face of every terror.

Yet even without Lycurgus saying so, I think you yourself will realize that such a person captured in war would not divulge any secret of Sparta when tortured by enemies; rather, mocking them as he is whipped, he would contend against the one hitting him until [that one] gives in first.

Anacharsis

[39] And Lycurgus himself, Solon, was he whipped at that age, or did he come up with such hot-headed youthful notions only once he was safely beyond the age of competition?

ΣΟΛΩΝ

Πρεσβύτης ἤδη ὢν ἔγραψε τοὺς νόμους αὐτοῖς Κρήτηθεν ἀφικόμενος. ἀποδεδημήκει δὲ παρὰ τοὺς Κρῆτας, ὅτι ἤκουεν εὐνομωτάτους εἶναι, Μίνωος τοῦ Διὸς νομοθετήσαντος ἐν αὐτοῖς.

ΑΝΑΧΑΡΣΙΣ

Τί οὖν, ὦ Σόλων, οὐχὶ καὶ σὺ ἐμιμήσω Λυκοῦργον καὶ μαστιγοῖς τοὺς νέους; καλὰ γὰρ καὶ ταῦτα καὶ ἄξια ὑμῶν ἐστιν.

ΣΟΛΩΝ

Ὅτι ἡμῖν ἱκανά, ὦ Ἀνάχαρσι, ταῦτα τὰ γυμνάσια οἰκεῖα ὄντα· ζηλοῦν δὲ τὰ ξενικὰ οὐ πάνυ ἀξιοῦμεν.

Solon

He was already an old man when he wrote these laws for them upon his return from Crete. He had visited the Cretans because he was hearing that they were the most law-abiding people, Minos, the son of Zeus,[34] having been their law-giver.

Anacharsis

Why then, Solon, did you not imitate Lycurgus and whip your young men? For these things are good and worthy of you.

Solon

Because, Anacharsis, these exercises are sufficient for us and also our own; we hardly deem it worthy to emulate those of strangers.

ΑΝΑΧΑΡΣΙΣ

Οὔκ; ἀλλὰ συνίῃς, οἶμαι, οἷόν τί ἐστι μαστιγοῦσθαι γυμνὸν ἄνω τὰς χεῖρας ἐπαίροντα μηδενὸς ἕνεκα ὠφελίμου ἢ αὐτῷ ἑκάστῳ ἢ κοινῇ τῇ πόλει. ὡς ἔγωγε ἤν ποτε ἐπιδημήσω τῇ Σπάρτῃ καθ᾽ ὃν καιρὸν ταῦτα δρῶσι, δοκῶ μοι τάχιστα καταλευσθήσεσθαι δημοσίᾳ πρὸς αὐτῶν, ἐπιγελῶν ἑκάστοις, ὁπόταν ὁρῶ τυπτομένους καθάπερ κλέπτας ἢ λωποδύτας ἤ τι ἄλλο τοιοῦτον ἐργασαμένους. ἀτεχνῶς γὰρ ἐλλεβόρου δεῖσθαί μοι δοκεῖ ἡ πόλις αὐτῶν καταγέλαστα ὑφ᾽ αὑτῆς πάσχουσα.

ΣΟΛΩΝ

[40] Μὴ ἐρήμην, ὦ γενναῖε, μηδὲ τῶν ἀνδρῶν ἀπόντων μόνος αὐτὸς λέγων οἴου κρατεῖν·

Anacharsis

No? Nonetheless you understand, I think, what a thing it is to be whipped naked while raising hands high for the sake of no benefit either for each individual himself or for the city in common. So, if I, for my part, should ever visit Sparta during a time when they are doing these things, it seems to me that I will be publicly stoned as soon as possible in their presence for laughing at each of them whenever I see them beaten exactly as robbers or petty thieves or others in those particular lines of work. For it seems to me the city is simply in need of hellebore[35] for suffering such mockeries at its own hands.

Solon

[40] Do not think, noble one, that you prevail by default[36] or are speaking alone with

ἔσται γάρ τις ὁ καὶ ὑπὲρ ἐκείνων σοι τὰ εἰκότα ἐν Σπάρτῃ ἀντερῶν.

Πλὴν ἀλλὰ ἐπείπερ ἐγὼ τὰ ἡμέτερά σοι διεξελήλυθα, σὺ δὲ οὐ πάνυ ἀρεσκομένῳ αὐτοῖς ἔοικας, οὐκ ἄδικα αἰτήσειν ἔοικα παρὰ σοῦ ὡς καὶ αὐτὸς ἐν τῷ μέρει διεξέλθῃς πρός με ὃν τρόπον ὑμεῖς οἱ Σκύθαι διασκεῖτε τοὺς νέους τοὺς παρ᾽ ὑμῖν καὶ οἷστισι γυμνασίοις ἀνατρέφετε καὶ ὅπως ὑμῖν ἄνδρες ἀγαθοὶ γίγνονται.

ΑΝΑΧΑΡΣΙΣ

Δικαιότατα μὲν οὖν, ὦ Σόλων, καὶ ἔγωγε διηγήσομαι τὰ Σκυθῶν νόμιμα, οὐ σεμνὰ ἴσως οὐδὲ καθ᾽ ὑμᾶς, οἵ γε οὐδὲ κατὰ κόρρης παταχθῆναι τολμήσαιμεν ἂν μίαν πληγήν· δειλοὶ γάρ ἐσμεν· ἀλλὰ εἰρήσεταί γε ὁποῖα ἂν

men absent, for in Sparta there will be someone to speak plausibly against you on behalf of these things.

Nevertheless, since I have gone through our customs, and you do not look like you are altogether pleased by them, it does not look like it would be unjust to demand this from you: that you also go through for me in detail the way you Scythians train your young men and with what exercises you bring them up and how they become good men for you.

Anacharsis

It would be most just indeed, Solon, and in fact I will describe the customs of the Scythians, which perhaps are neither majestic nor on your level—for we at least would not dare to be struck on the cheek with even one blow since we are cowards. Yet whatever

εἴη. εἰς αὔριον μέντοι, εἰ δοκεῖ, ὑπερβαλώμεθα τὴν συνουσίαν, ὡς ἅ τε αὐτὸς ἔφης ἔτι μᾶλλον ἐννοήσαιμι καθ᾽ ἡσυχίαν ἅ τε χρὴ εἰπεῖν συναγάγοιμι τῇ μνήμῃ ἐπελθών. τὸ δὲ νῦν ἔχον ἀπίωμεν ἐπὶ τούτοις· ἑσπέρα γὰρ ἤδη.

sort they [our customs] might be, they will indeed be told. But if you agree, let us put off our conversation until tomorrow. That way I might quietly reflect further on what you yourself said and gather together the necessary responses by going over them in my memory. For the moment let us part on these terms, since it is already evening.

GLOSSARY

Antagonist (ἀνταγωνιστής). This term for a competitor or opponent should not be confused with "enemies" (*polemioi, echthroi*) or "those hostile" (*dusmenees*). In the context of **competition** (*agōn*) and **exertion** (*ponos*), antagonists benefit rather than harm one another by providing a welcome challenge. In §1 Anacharsis is astonished by the initial friendliness and subsequent ferocity between competitors.

Ardor (θερμός). Refers literally to heat, but among ancient Greek medical thinkers like Galen and Hippocrates, it was linked with masculinity and health.

Arms (ὅπλα). Refers especially to large shields carried by hoplites, but also to armor and

defensive weapons. Solon argues that athletic training prepares young men for war, but Anacharsis thinks it is **pointless** and that professional military training is what matters. Ancient Greek athletic festivals included a footrace called the *hoplitodromos*, in which competitors wore helmets and carried shields, but did not fight.

Beautiful (κάλλος). Beauty in ancient Greek thought combines aesthetic and moral qualities. When Solon describes the city's traditions and its management as *kallista* (most beautiful) in §14, he refers not only to their functioning well but also to their aesthetic appeal. In §30 he says that the "height of the city's well-being" comes from youth developing **zeal** for "what is most beautiful."

Best (ἄριστος). Being the best in terms of **excellence** was central to athletic culture in ancient Greece. Solon argues that **training** and **competition** produce the best citizens and the best political organization.

Boxing (πυγμή). Ancient Greek boxing lacked weight classes, time limits, and padded gloves, which made it the most dangerous of the "heavy events"—so called because larger, heavier athletes excelled at them. Bouts were held outdoors under the midday sun and continued until one of the boxers conceded by raising a finger or was unable to go on. Athletes wrapped their hands and wrists in leather thongs called *himantes*.

Competition (ἀγών). Denotes an assembly of both **spectators** and participants gathered for a struggle or conflict, including tests of sports, drama, and trials. The Olympics and other athletic festivals are referred to even in modern Greek as *agōnes* and not "games." The seriousness of Greek sport is discussed in §32.

Contest (ἅμιλλα). Refers more specifically than *agōn* to a competition for superiority. Anacharsis says in §32 that those seeking *aretē* require a dangerous *hamilla* against those hostile to them.

Discus (δίσκος). In Homer (*Odyssey* 8.196-98), Odysseus proves his **excellence** with an amazing discus throw. In ancient athletics the discus throw for distance was part of the pentathlon but not a stand-alone event. *Diskoi* differed in size and Solon says they were used in the **gymnasium** to strengthen and tone the upper body (§27).

Dust (κόνις). Refers both to the sand and dirt in which athletes trained and to the substance they sprinkled on their bodies after applying **olive oil**—perhaps to provide a better grip (§2). According to Philostratus' *Gymnasticus* §56, different kinds of dust had different uses ranging from the disinfectant to the aesthetic. Meanwhile, when wrestlers won a contest unopposed (because all of their competitors withdrew rather than face them), this prestigious victory was called "dustless" (*akoniti*).

Education (παιδεία). Refers not just to schooling, but to participation in a culture designed

to make people as good as possible. Solon describes *paideia* as a process of ordering and cultivation that combines athletic training with orientation towards **excellence** by means of poetry, moral maxims, theater, and laws (§§20–22). He also demonstrates a continued willingness to learn by suggesting that Anacharsis' challenges may educate him and benefit the city (§17).

Effort (κάματος). Is linked to the **exertion** or resulting fatigue associated with noble achievements or feats called *athla.* It can refer to the pangs of childbirth, or as in §8, to the efforts of a god. In fact, statues of "weary" gods and heroes such as Heracles were commonly found in gymnasiums, probably to inspire the noble efforts of trainees.

Endurance (καρτερία). Has both physical and psychological dimensions. It was the object of the Spartan whipping contest discussed in §38. Most ancient sports required endurance. Boxing, wrestling, and *pankration* had no

rounds or time limits. The marathon is a modern invention, but there was a "long race" called *dolichos* run back and forth on the *stadion* (track) up to twenty-four times for a total of about 5,000 meters.

Excellence (ἀρετή). Often translated "virtue," *aretē* is the quality that makes anything excellent in its kind. Athletic contests were thought to reveal and celebrate *aretē*, which showed our closeness to heroes and gods. In Ancient Greek philosophy *aretē* was a moral condition that enabled good action. Anacharsis asks specifically how gymnastic training contributes to *aretē* (§18), and Solon describes a holistic program in which poetry and drama describing past deeds of excellence inspire youth to pursue similar excellence through sport (§21–22).

Exercise (γύμνασμα, γυμνασία). As in English, it can refer to athletic exercises such as wrestling or running, as well as to practice in other disciplines, including rhetoric. See also **gymnasium**.

Exertion (πόνος). Can refer to toil and even to the pain that results from it, but in a gymnastic context it is the exertion needed to pursue success (§10). In §35, Anacharsis suggests that athletic exertion is a **pointless** waste of strength, but Solon explains that a person's power actually increases as a result of hard training.

Fitness (εὐεξία). A condition reached through activity that promotes good performance of that activity. For Aristotle, **excellence** was a kind of moral fitness produced by doing good actions that was productive of more good actions.

Freedom (ἐλευθερία). Refers to personal autonomy and also marks the political boundary between the free population of a city, who were allowed to use the **gymnasium**, and enslaved people who were explicitly prohibited from oiling themselves for exercise there.

Gymnasium (γυμνάσιον). From *gymnos* (naked), the term refers to a place for naked exercise.

Minimally, it was a park-like space with shade and access to water. In its monumentalized form, known archaeologically from the 4th century BCE on (e.g., at Amphipolis, Delphi, and Eretria among others), the complex often included a peristyle building with rooms surrounding an open courtyard, called a *palaistra*, from *palē*, the word for wrestling. Solon and Anacharsis seem to go inside the *palaistra* to sit on stone seats in the *exedra*, a room that opened onto the courtyard.

Happiness (εὐδαιμονία). The concept in Greek goes beyond a subjective feeling to encompass objective criteria such as prosperity, good-fortune, social acceptance, and thriving. Solon defends the value of sport as a contribution to individual happiness and the happiness of the city as a whole (§15).

Hyperbolic Training (ὑπερβολὴν, ἄσκησις). Progressive overload training, as we call it today, was associated in ancient Greece with Milo of Croton, who is said to have lifted a calf on his

shoulders every day until it became a bull. Training with weights is mentioned in §27.

Imitation (μίμησις). In §21, Solon says that hearing about feats of **excellence** in song and witnessing them in the theater inspires youth to *mimēsis*, that is, to imitate such models and thereby strive for the kind of excellence that is worthy of song. This is consistent with the idea that athletics are a *mimēsis* of the heroic *athla* in epic poetry, with athletic *athla* deserving corresponding celebration in *epinician* (victory) poetry.

Javelin (ἀκόντιον). A contest throwing spears (*engchē*) is attested in Homer's *Iliad* (23.884–97), our earliest account of sport. The lighter javelin was part of the pentathlon, rather than a stand-alone event. It was thrown for distance, except in the Panathenaia where ephebes threw it at a target. A leather thong called an *ankylē* may have been used to impart spin, which might account for the hissing sound mentioned in §31.

Jumping (ὑπεράλλομαι). Long-jumping (*halma*) was part of the pentathlon competition; but in §8 Solon uses the term *hyperallesthai*, which just means "jumping over." There is no evidence of a high-jump in ancient sports, so this probably refers to a kind of training. The *halma* was performed using hand-held weights called *halteres* which, according to Aristotle (*Progression of Animals* 705a16-17), helped athletes jump farther.

Love of Honor (φιλοτιμία; φιλοτιμέομαι). This describes the motivation to distinguish oneself and earn the admiration of one's peers, especially through athletic and social competition. In §14 Solon places "the love of honor (*philotimia*) with which we contend (*philotimoumetha*)" at the center of successful city management.

Lyceum (Λύκειον). The setting of *Anacharsis* is a **gymnasium** in central Athens that took its name from a neighboring temple dedicated to Apollo *Lykeios*. This *gymnasion* is identified

by Plato as a favorite hangout of the philosopher Socrates, and it would be recognized by Lucian's readers as the home of Aristotle's school.

Lycurgus (Λυκοῦργος). The founding lawgiver of Sparta, which makes him Solon's counterpart. He was famed for his social and political reforms, which included gymnastic education for both males and females, plus the harsh athletic rituals described in §38–9. By Lucian's time, the sites of such rituals had become popular tourist attractions.

Mind (ψυχή). Sometimes translated as "soul," *psychē* was understood as the feature of the human person that made them alive and included their thoughts, emotions, and appetites. Solon describes an education in which the mind must be trained along with the body.

Naked (γυμνός). Can refer literally to the state of being unclothed or metaphorically to states of poverty or vulnerability. In *Anacharsis,* the

term appears in reference to speeches at a trial, contrasting the "naked truth" with one "dressed up in words" (§19). Athletic performance, in a parallel way, was connected with truth, and it is not by accident that Socrates's philosophical undressing of young men in Plato's dialogues is sometimes set in the *apodyterion* (undressing room) of a **gymnasium** or *palaistra.* See §36.

Olive Oil (ἔλαιον). Before exercising in the **gymnasium** or competing in athletics, trainees covered their bodies in olive oil, which was offered in great quantities at public or a benefactor's expense. There is no consensus as to its purpose, but the benefits of anointing (*aleiphein*) were probably psychological as well as practical—not unlike "suiting up" in a locker room today. It may have had a religious dimension as well, for sacred olive oil was offered as a prize at the Panathenaia (§7). Solon also claims that it makes skin more supple and durable (§24) and increases grip

strength by making opponents slippery (§28). See **dust**.

Pankration (παγκράτιον). A combination of wrestling and boxing similar to mixed martial arts, in which only the gouging of eyes and biting and were prohibited. **Victory** was earned when a competitor signaled submission by raising a finger. This "heavy event" was violent and sometimes bloody, but considered less dangerous in antiquity than boxing.

Pointless (μάτην). Ancient Greek philosophers counseled people to avoid "pointless" activities like accumulating wealth and to focus instead on the things that really make life better, especially **excellence**. Anacharsis repeatedly criticizes athletic activity and suffering as *matēn*, suggesting that they serve no worthwhile purpose. Solon counters that both the activities and the **zeal** they inspire are not *matēn* because they lead to **happiness**.

Prizes (ἆθλα). Though lucrative prizes were offered at secondary events, the most prestigious festivals awarded only crowns of sacred vegetation. Solon says such prizes are primarily symbolic (§10), and he argues that the most important crown is made of **happiness** (§15). *Athla* connect sport to a larger culture of heroic struggle and achievement. The term *athla* also refers to the feats or "labors" of heroes such as Heracles; in fact, the words *athlete* and *athletics* derive from this root.

Spectator (θεατής). The presence of spectators is built into the Greek idea of **competition** (*agōn*). Olympia's stadium could seat up to 40,000, bringing people from different and even warring cities together to worship common gods. Anacharsis thinks the naked violence and suffering of sport is only made worse by the gaze of spectators, who should be attending to more serious things (§11). Solon argues that watching sports and drama in the theater is educational because they

inspire the pursuit of **excellence** (§12, §23, §36).

Sweat (ἱδρώς). Similar to English usage, sweat can refer metaphorically to a hard effort or struggle, as well as literally to perspiration. A saying goes back to Hesiod (*Works and Days* 289–90) that "the gods put sweat before *aretē*," meaning that **exertion** is required to achieve **excellence.** The sweat produced in **gymnasiums,** along with the oil and dust, was scraped from trainees' bodies using a strigil (*stlengis*) and collected for medicinal purposes as a substance called *gloios.*

Tone (τόνος). The term relates to the tension in muscles or the strings of a musical instrument that produces energy. Good tone is the result of proper "tuning," i.e., stretching and tightening, which can be understood mechanically or psychologically, as in the "attunement of the *psychē.*"

Training (ἄσκησις). Can refer to various kinds of structured exercise, not only gymnastic

and athletic exercise. Indeed, the term later takes on religious connotations and becomes the root of our term "asceticism." Here, the debate concerns the best type of *askēsis.* Solon argues for the athletic form (§15), but Anacharsis insists that only serious *askēsis* with arms can lead to **freedom** and **happiness** (§31).

Victory (νίκη). *Nikē* refers to the goddess of victory, as well as victory itself, in athletics, war, or any other contest. The value of victory lies in the social recognition of one's worthiness (§10, 36) and not the **prizes** of apples and leafy crowns that Anacharsis ridicules (§9, 13).

Violence (ὕβρις). Often mistranslated as "excessive pride," *hubris* refers rather to wanton or rash violence, insolence, or outrage directed at a person. Anacharsis worries that boxing, wrestling, and *pankration* involve *hubris,* which seems harmful to practitioners and spectators alike (§11), but Solon argues that athletes fight not for the sake of violence (§7),

but rather to achieve useful ends that ultimately discourage *hubris* (§30).

Why (τίνος ἕνεκα). When Anacharsis asks at the beginning of the dialogue "why" (*tinos heneka,* i.e., "to what end," "for the sake of what") the young men are training, it can be interpreted as a philosophical question about the role of sport in achieving a good life both for oneself and one's city. The dialogue essentially discusses the question "Why sports?"

Wrestling (πάλη). A basic form of exercise, even for children, as well as a serious Olympic event for individuals and part of the pentathlon. There were no weight classes in ancient Greek wrestling, so competitive wrestlers like Milo of Croton tended to be large and wrestling was considered one of the "heavy events." Matches began from an upright position and were scored according to "falls," e.g., forcing an opponent's back or shoulders to touch the ground.

Zeal (σπουδή). Connotes both the eagerness and seriousness of the Athenians' approach to sport, which Anacharsis denounces as **pointless** (§9). Solon says it has social benefits (§14), arguing that theater (§22), sport (§30), and even cockfights (§37) inspire zeal for the **excellence** displayed there.

NOTES

Introduction

1 See Francesca Mestre, "Anacharsis, the Wise Man from Abroad," *Lexis Poetica Retorica E Comunicaciones Nella Tradizione Classica* 17 (2003): 303–317, who notes that Diogenes Laertius' biography of Anacharsis (1.103–104) describes the Scythian's friendship with Solon and his perplexity over Greek athletics.

2 A gymnasium was an outdoor area used for athletic exercise (*gymnasia*), which in ancient Greece was typically performed in the nude, "*gymnos*" being the Greek term for "naked."

3 The 6th-century-BCE philosopher Pythagoras not only lectured in Croton's gymnasium but apparently trained athletes there as he had in his native Samos—initiating a dynasty of Olympic champions that included Milo.

Socrates, of course, was famous for frequenting the *gymnasion*, and Plato set many of his dialogues there. For an analysis of the evidence, see Heather Reid, "Plato the Gymnasiarch," in *ΦΙΛΕΛΛΗΝ: Essays for Stephen G. Miller*, edited by D. Katsonopoulou and E. Partida (Athens: Helike Society, 2016), 171–186.

4 See Tim Whitmarsh, *The Second Sophistic* (Oxford: Oxford University Press, 2005).

5 See R. Bracht Branham, *Unruly Eloquence: Lucian and the Comedy of Traditions* (Cambridge, MA: Harvard University Press, 1989), especially the analysis of *Anacharsis*, 82–102.

6 Says Branham, *Unruly Eloquence*, 102, the purpose of Lucian's dialectical humor "is not to test [each proposition's] truth value, which would make little sense, but to create comically unorthodox perspectives from which to interrogate their traditional meanings."

7 It is worth noting that by Lucian's time in the 2nd century CE, there were many professional athletes who earned a living by participating in regional games with lucrative prizes; however, the

most prestigious festivals, such as the Olympic Games, still offered only leafy crowns to victors. See Stephen G. Miller, *Ancient Greek Athletics* (New Haven, CT: Yale University Press, 2004), 129.

8 The main text is Johan Huizinga, *Homo Ludens: A Study of the Play Element in Culture* (Boston: Beacon Press, [1944] 1955). David Konstan argues that failure to comprehend the nature of games as play is Lucian's message in this dialogue, in "Anacharsis the Roman, or Reality vs. Play," in *Lucian of Samosata, Greek Writer and Roman Citizen,* edited by Francesca Mestre and Pilar Gómez Cardó (Barcelona: Edicions Universitat, 2010), 191–97.

9 The heroic virtue of athletes themselves was also celebrated in statues with inscriptions. On athletics as *mimēsis* of heroic *athla*, see Gregory Nagy, *The Ancient Greek Hero in 24 Hours* (Cambridge, MA: Harvard University Press, 2013), esp. 1§41. On the educational effect, see Heather L. Reid, "Performing Virtue: Athletic *Mimēsis* in Platonic Education," in *Politics and*

Performance in Western Greece, edited by H. Reid, D. Tanasi, and S. Kimbell (Sioux City, IA: Parnassos Press, 2017), 260–71.

10 This story may recall the real massacre of men in a gymnasium by Ptolemy VII in 126 BCE (Val. Max. 9.2.ext.5).

11 See Matthew Evans, "Architectural and Spatial Features of Plato's *Gymnasia* and *Palaistrai*," in *Athletics, Gymnastics, and Agon in Plato*, edited by H. Reid, M. Ralkowski, and C. Zoller (Sioux City, IA: Parnassos Press, 2020), 31–50.

12 Concludes Jason König, *Athletics and Literature in the Roman Empire* (Cambridge: Cambridge University Press, 2005), 95: "Lucian dramatizes the question of whether unthinking reception of archaizing tradition within the contemporary world, of the kind Solon, for the most part seems to represent, or tenacious interrogation of it, is the more properly Hellenic response. In the process, he ingeniously undermines the certainties of both his interlocutors, and humorously challenges his readers to re-examine the significance of their own preconceptions."

Anacharsis, or About Naked Exercise

1 This sentence contains several technical wrestling terms, which were also used metaphorically in other contexts, including philosophical and rhetorical debate. Pollux 3.155 lists wrestling terms educated men should know. See Michael B. Poliakoff, *Studies in the Terminology of Greek Combat Sport*, Ph.D. Diss. University of Michigan, 1981; Debra Hawhee, *Bodily Arts: Rhetoric and Athletics in Ancient Greece* (Austin: University of Texas Press, 2004), 34–39.

2 "Heavy events," such as boxing, *pankration*, and sometimes wrestling (which was usually decided by three falls), continued until one competitor signaled concession.

3 The "man in charge" is either a coach (*gymnastēs*) or an official, called *alytēs*, *mastigophoros*, or *rhabdophoros* because they carried a whip or switch to restrain or punish competitors.

4 In Lucian, "madness" (*mania*) is often viewed as a kind of infectious enthusiasm or

disease that must be treated by reason. Solon responds to Anacharsis that although he will find training contagious, it is not irrational madness, but useful to individuals and society.

5 An *akinakēs* is a short knife worn in the belt, typical of Scythian dress.

6 The statue described was attributed to Praxiteles and was copied so frequently that there is an "Apollo Lyceus" type.

7 On the various crowns awarded at the Panhellenic Games, see Oscar Broneer, "The Isthmian Victory Crown," *American Journal of Archaeology* 66, no. 3 (1962): 259–63. https://doi.org/10.2307/501451.

8 The traditional prize at Delphi was a laurel crown, but in the Imperial period when Lucian is writing, apples from a sacred grove were also awarded to victors. See Georges Roux, *Delphes: son Oracle et ses Dieux*, (Paris: Belles Lettres, 1976), 172–173, who suggests that this practice recalls the apples offered to Apollo by the Parnassian nymphs after his fight against Pytho.

9 The prize is mentioned by Aristotle, *Constitution of Athens* 60, and evidenced by the many "Panathenaic" prize vases that survive. The sacred grove may have been at the Academy according to a scholion on Sophocles's *Oedipus at Colonus* (K 701), and the Suda (s.v. *moriai*).

10 Anacharsis' sarcasm here reflects Socratic-style irony. He makes readers question the value of sport by contrasting the practical worthlessness of the prizes with the competitive zeal of athletes, and of benefactors (*euergetes*) who tried to outdo each other in terms of civic munificence by sponsoring the contests.

11 Uncertainty of outcome is recognized as a foundational value in ancient and modern sport alike. For an explanation, see Heather Reid, *Introduction to the Philosophy of Sport* 2nd ed. (Lanham, MD: Rowman and Littlefield, 2023), 6, 27, 278.

12 Here Lucian plays on the double meaning of *athlios* (miserable). See Galen *Protrepticus* 11: "In terms of bodily health, it is clear that no

group is more miserable than athletes. Thus, someone might appropriately call athletes miserable (*athlios*)—either the term 'athletes' comes from the term *athlios* 'miserable' or the term *athlios* comes from the condition of athletes—or perhaps both have a common source in the term 'misery' (*athliotēs*)."

13 On the connection between gymnasiums and happiness (*eudaimonia*), see Diodorus Siculus 4.30.1: 5.15.2: κατασκεύασε δὲ καὶ γυμνάσια καὶ θεῶν ναοὺς καὶ τἄλλα πάντα τὰ πρὸς βίον ἀνθρώπων εὐδαίμονα ("and they built gymnasiums and temples of the gods and all the rest of the things for a happy life of human beings.")

14 Scythians wore pointed felt caps, also called Phyrigian caps, that would have stood out as the mark of a foreigner in Athens. The Paris 2024 Olympic mascots were modeled on these caps.

15 Pnyx is a hill in central Athens where the democratic assemblies met.

16 On the monument of the Eponymous Heroes, which represented the tribes of Athens,

see T. L. Shear, "The Monument of the Eponymous Heroes in the Athenian Agora," *Hesperia* 39 (1970): 145–222.

17 *Barbaros* originally referred to anyone who does not speak Greek.

18 Athenians claimed to be *autochthonous*, i.e., "sprung from the earth," because they had always lived in Athens and not migrated there from elsewhere, in contrast to the nomad.

19 Ancient Greek gymnasia often had covered walkways and rooms with stone seats where lectures and philosophical conversations took place. See Vitruvius, *On Architecture* 5.11.1-5.

20 At the end of §17, Solon had called Anacharsis *barbaros* and *xenos*, i.e., a "non-Hellenic stranger." Here Anacharsis, who does speak Greek, refers to himself as a *barbaros* who cannot follow complicated arguments. Perhaps this is an ironic statement that uses the term's later pejorative connotations to emphasize his critical distance.

21 There is a connection here between the nudity of the athlete, whose *aretē* is proven through performance, and the idea of "naked truth" which is not "dressed up" in rhetoric or deception. See Heather Reid and Georgios Mouratidis, "Naked Virtue: Ancient Athletic Nudity and the Olympic Ethos of *Arete*," in *Olympika: The International Journal of Olympic Studies* 29 (2020): 29–55.

22 By using the term *sunousia*, Lucian may be very discreetly referring to erotic educational relationships between older and younger men that were common in Solon's Athens. For more on these relationships and their connection to athletics, see Thomas F. Scanlon, *Eros and Greek Athletics* (Oxford: Oxford University Press, 2002).

23 In Lucian's time, the term *sophist* refers primarily to the great rhetoricians and educators of 5th century Greece, without the negative connotations familiar from Plato.

24 The costumes of tragic actors included elevated boots called *kothorni* and masks with

fixed expressions and big openings for mouths, which Anacharsis refers to as "helmets."

25 The *aulos* was a double pipe wind instrument, used in both theaters and gymnasiums. See Wendy J. Rashke, "*Aulos* and Athlete: The Function of the Flute-Player in Greek Athletics," *Arete: the Journal of Sport Literature* 2.2 (1985): 177–200.

26 The Greek *leukos* means "white," but here it refers to the paleness associated with weakness and illness.

27 "Tribute" in this context refers to payments in exchange for protection or in acknowledgment of submission.

28 Contests in arms are recorded in Homer (*Iliad* 23.799–825) and existed in gymnasiums and festivals. Plato's *Laws* 830e recommends moderately dangerous war games for children as a way of testing their courage.

29 Eumolpus, king of Thrace, attacked Athens and was defeated by its legendary king Erechtheus. Hippolyta, queen of the Amazons,

was defeated by the Athenian hero and king Theseus.

30 The Greek *houtinos heneka* is ambiguous between "for the sake of what" and "for the sake of whom." We translate "to what end" to capture Solon's answer, which emphasizes the benefits for both individuals and communities.

31 On the question of mandatory viewing of cockfights in Athens, see Eric Csapo, "Cockfights, Contradictions and the Mythopoetics of Ancient Greek Culture," in *Arts: The Journal of the Sydney University Arts Association* 28 (2006): 9–41.

32 Solon is referring to Spartan *agōgē*, which involved team and individual contests in toughness and endurance. His description of the contest in which teams of ephebes tried to push each other off an artificial island resembles that of Pausanias, *Description of Greece*, 3.14.8.

33 The whipping contest in honor of Artemis Orthia was much discussed in antiquity. For a list of testimonia, see Nigel Kennell, *The*

Gymnasium of Virtue (Chapel Hill: University of North Carolina Press, 1995), appendix 1.

34 After his death, Minos became one of the judges in the Underworld.

35 Hellebore was an herbal treatment for insanity.

36 The term *erēmēn* refers to winning a case by default because the opposing party does not show up in court.

FURTHER READING

Greek Edition of *Anacharsis*

Luciani Opera II, ed. M.D. Macleod. Oxford: Oxford University Press, 2008.

Translations of *Anacharsis*

Caccia, Gianni. Luciano di Samosata, *Dialoghi Scitici*. Napoli: Senecio, 2021.

Fowler, H. W. and F. G. Fowler. *Lucian* vol. ii. Oxford: Clarendon Press, 1905.

Harmon, A. M. *Lucian* vol. iv. Cambridge, MA: Harvard University Press, 1925.

Ozanam, Anne-Marie. *Lucien, Oeuvres Completes.* Paris: Belles Lettres, 2018.

Stocking, Charles H., and Susan A. Stephens, *Ancient Greek Athletics: Primary Sources in Translation.* Oxford: Oxford University Press, 2021.

Studies on Lucian

Branham, R. Bracht. *Unruly Eloquence: Lucian and the Comedy of Traditions.* Cambridge, MA: Harvard University Press, 1989.

Kuin, Inger. *Lucian's Laughing Gods.* Ann Arbor: University of Michigan Press, 2023.

Mestre, Francesca and Pilar Gómez Cardó, eds. *Lucian of Samosata, Greek Writer and Roman Citizen.* Barcelona: Edicions Universitat, 2010.

Studies in Ancient Greek Athletics

Bertolín Cebrián, Reyes. *The Athlete in the Ancient Greek World.* Norman: University of Oklahoma Press, 2020.

Golden, Mark. *Greek Sport and Social Status.* Austin: University of Texas Press, 2008.

Hawhee, Debra. *Bodily Arts: Rhetoric and Athletics in Ancient Greece.* Austin: University of Texas Press, 2004.

Kennell, Nigel M. *The Gymnasium of Virtue: Education & Culture in Ancient Sparta.*

Chapel Hill, NC: University of North Carolina Press, 1995.

König, Jason. *Athletics and Literature in the Roman Empire.* Cambridge: Cambridge University Press, 2005.

Lunt, David. *The Crown Games of Ancient Greece.* Fayetteville: University of Arkansas Press, 2022.

Miller, Stephen G., ed. Arete: *Greek Sports from Ancient Sources.* Berkeley: University of California Press, 1991.

Nagy, Gregory. *Ancient Greek Heroes, Athletes, Poetry.* Cambridge, MA: Harvard University Press, 2024.

Newby, Zahra. *Greek Athletics in the Roman World: Victory and Virtue*. Oxford: Oxford University Press, 2005.

Poliakoff, Michael B. *Combat Sports in the Ancient World.* New Haven: Yale University Press, 1987.

Scanlon, Thomas F. *Eros and Greek Athletics.* New York: Oxford University Press, 2002.

——— ed., *Sport in the Greek and Roman Worlds.* 2 vols. Oxford: Oxford University Press, 2014.

Spivey, Nigel. *The Ancient Olympics: A History.* Oxford: Oxford University Press, 2004.

Ancient Greek Philosophy of Sport

Dombrowski, Daniel. *Contemporary Athletics and Ancient Greek Ideals.* Chicago: University of Chicago Press, 2009.

Kenyon, Erik. *Philosophy at the Gymnasium.* Ithaca, NY: Cornell University Press, 2024.

Reid, Heather L. *Athletics and Philosophy in the Ancient World: Contests of Virtue*. New York: Routledge, 2011.

———. *Ancient Olympic Philosophy: Sport, Athletes, Excellence, Education, Women, Beauty, Peace.* Sioux City, IA: Parnassos Press, 2024.

Studies in the Philosophy of Sport

Guttman, Allen. *From Ritual to Record: The Nature of Modern Sport.* New York: Columbia University Press, 1978.

Huizinga, Johan. *Homo Ludens: A Study of the Play Element in Culture*. Boston: Beacon Press, 1955.

Hyland, Drew. *Philosophy of Sport.* New York: Paragon, 1990.

Reid, Heather L. *Introduction to the Philosophy of Sport.* 2nd ed. Lanham, MD: Rowman and Littlefield, 2023.

———. *Olympic Philosophy: The Ideas and Ideals behind the Ancient and Modern Olympic Games.* Sioux City, IA: Parnassos Press, 2020.

Simon, Robert L. *Fair Play: The Ethics of Sport.* New York: Routledge, 2015.

Suits, Bernard. *The Grasshopper: Games, Life, and Utopia*. 2nd ed. Peterborough, Ontario: Broadview, [1978] 2005.

ACKNOWLEDGMENTS

We would like to thank for their assistance Charles H. Stocking, Jean-Manuel Roubineau, R.J. Barnes, Onno M. van Nijf, Tarik Orliczek, Giorgos Mouratidis, Gregory Nagy, Paul Cartledge, Stamatia Dova, Matthew Evans, Paul Mitsis, Dylan Baldwin, and Jurgen R. Gatt.

Special thanks also to Rob Tempio, Chloe Coy, and Jill Harris from Princeton University Press.